Ogham:
The Ancient Celtic Alphabet

Origins, Evolution, Mythology, Meanings, Divination, and Magic

Matthew Leigh Embleton

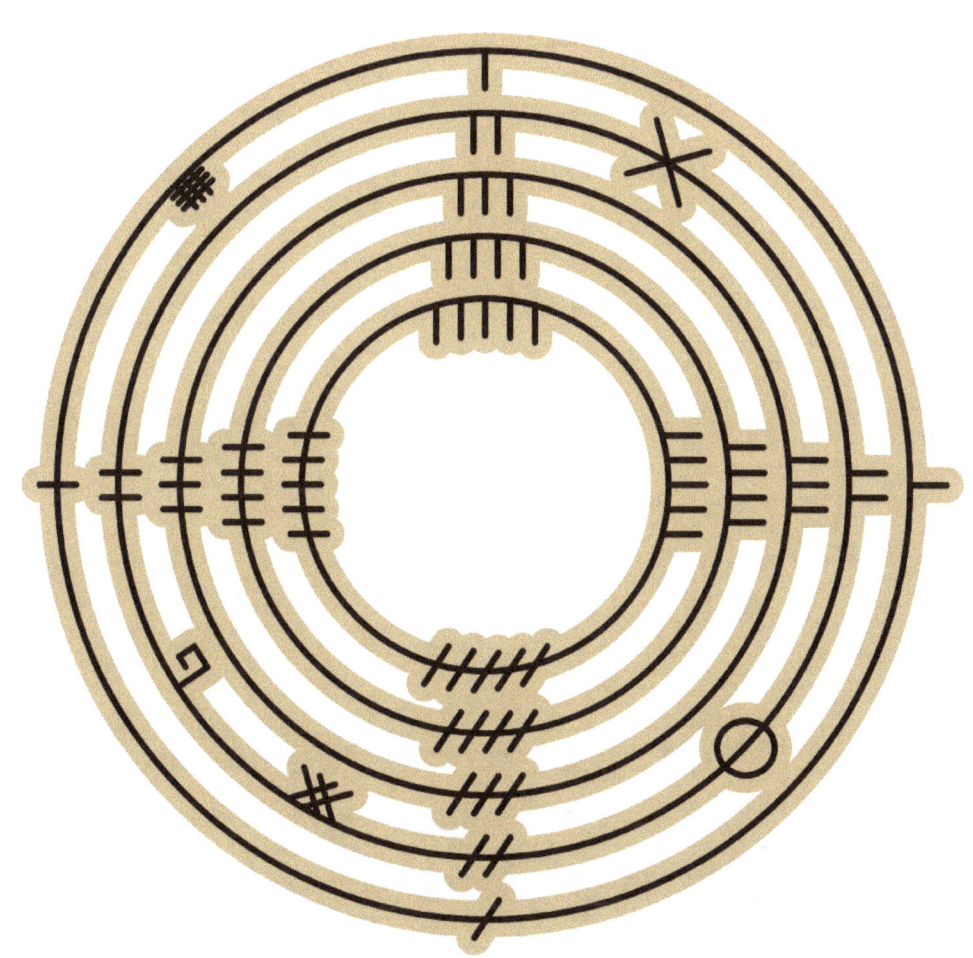

Copyright ©2021 Matthew Leigh Embleton. All rights reserved.

Ogham

1 Origins and Evolution 1
   1.1   The Origin of the word 'Ogham' 1
   1.2   Original Inscriptions 1
   1.3   The Language of Ogham 1
       1.3.1   Archaic Irish 1
       1.3.2   Old Irish 1
       1.3.3   Insular Celtic Language Timeline 2
   1.4   *Beith-Luis-Fearn*: 'Orthodox' Ogham 3
   1.5   *Beith-Luis-Fearn*: 'Scholastic' Ogham and the '*Forfeda*' 4
   1.6   *Beith-Luis-Fearn*: 'Scholastic' Ogham: Horizontal 5
2 The Book of Ballymote 6
   2.1   *In Lebor Ogaim* (The Book of Ogams) 6
   2.2   *Auraicept na n-Éces* (The Scholar's Primer) 18
3 *Bríatharogaim*: Meanings 19
4 Mythology 22
   4.1   *Lebor Gabála Érenn*: The Book of the Taking of Ireland 22
   4.2   Ogma: The Father of Ogham 24
   4.3   *Auraicept na n-Éces* (The Scholar's Primer) 25
   4.4   *Tochmarc Étaíne* (The Wooing of Étaín / Éadaoin) 26
5 The Celtic Calendar 27
   5.1   The Coligny Calendar 27
   5.2   The 'Wheel of Year' 28
6 The Celtic Revival and the Pagan Revival 31
   6.1   R. A. S. Macalister 31
   6.2   Robert Graves 32
   6.3   Ogham Tree Meanings 34
   6.4   The Celtic Tree Calendar 35
7 Divination 37
   7.1   Deciding how many letters 37
   7.2   Distinguishing which way up the letters are 39
   7.3   Reversed letters 39
   7.4   Selecting what material to use 44
   7.5   Types of reading 48
   7.6   Casting 51
   7.7   Meanings for Divination 52
8 Magic 55
   8.1   Meanings for Magic 55
9 Inscriptions 58
   9.1   Common Features 58
   9.2   Ireland 58
   9.3   Wales 63
   9.4   England 64
   9.5   Isle of Man 66
   9.6   Scotland 68

Cover: '*Fege Find* - Fionn's Window', image by the author

Images in this book are the work of the author, except those in the public domain under Wikipedia Creative Commons where specified.

Acknowledgments

I have long been fascinated by languages and history, and I am very grateful to the special people in my life who have supported and encouraged me in my work. Thank you for believing in me. You know who you are.

Introduction

Ogham is an ancient Celtic writing system, alphabet, or cipher that was primarily designed to inscript Archaic Irish (sometimes called Primitive Irish), later Old Irish, and some Pictish and Old Welsh.

As well as having origins documented in the fields of history, linguistics, and archaeology, it also has a history of magic and mythology in Ancient Celtic Religion or Celtic Paganism.

Since the 20th century, there has been a revival of interest in this and other ancient polytheistic religions and spiritual practices by a growing number of Pagan or Neo-Pagan communities across the world.

It is the aim of this book to provide the bigger picture about where these symbols have come from, how they have developed, how they have been used, and how their use has evolved over two thousand years.

1 Origins and Evolution

1.1 The Origin of the word 'Ogham'

The origin of the word ogham is uncertain, but there are several theories:

- It comes from the Irish *og-úaim* ('point-seam'), referring to the seam made by the point of a sharp weapon, or simply 'grooved writing'.
- It comes from *'Ogma'*, the Celtic god of speech, writing, language, and poetry who, according to Celtic Mythology, is said to have devised the writing system.

1.2 Original Inscriptions

The earliest known surviving inscriptions of ogham are found on standing stones in Ireland (Kerry, Cork, Waterford), Wales (Pembrokeshire), Cornwall, Devon, the Isle of Man, and Scotland. They have been dated as far back as 300 CE but, some scholars believe that the development and use of ogham can be dated back even further to the first century BCE.

The inscriptions are carved from the bottom of the stone upwards, onto the *droim* or *faobhar* (edge), which acts as the centre line or stem of each character. The stones were raised as monuments, cenotaphs, tombstones, or markers documenting land ownership. As well as its use on large standing stones, ogham was also carved on to smaller items made of wood or metal, to convey messages, record poetry, or to mark ownership of the item that had been carved onto, and also for magical uses.

1.3 The Language of Ogham

1.3.1 Archaic Irish

Indo European	Proto Celtic	Insular Celtic	Goidelic	Archaic Irish
4000 BCE	1300 BCE	500 BCE	1 BCE	300 CE
1300 BCE	800 BCE	1 BCE	300 CE	600 CE

Much of what we know about Archaic Irish (sometimes called 'Primitive Irish') is from the ogham inscriptions found dated between 300 and 600 CE.

1.3.2 Old Irish

Indo European	Proto Celtic	Insular Celtic	Goidelic	Archaic Irish	Old Irish
4000 BCE	1300 BCE	500 BCE	1 BCE	300 CE	500 CE
1300 BCE	800 BCE	1 BCE	300 CE	600 CE	900 CE

It has also been possible for linguists to distinguish the differences between Archaic Irish and Old Irish by comparing the ogham inscriptions with the written texts that emerged centuries later.

1.3.3 Insular Celtic Language Timeline

4000 – 1300 BCE	Indo-European						
1300 – 800 BCE	Proto-Celtic						
800 BCE	Celtic						
700 BCE							
600 BCE							
500 BCE	Insular Celtic						
400 BCE							
300 BCE							
200 BCE							
100 BCE							
1	Goidelic			Brythonic			
200							
400	Archaic / Primitive Irish	Pictish	Ivernic	Common Brittonic			
500							
600	Old Irish			Western Brittonic	Southwestern Brittonic		
700							
1000	Middle Irish		Cumbric	Old Welsh	Old Cornish	Old Breton	
1100							
1200		Early Modern Irish			Middle Welsh	Middle Cornish	Middle Breton
1400							
1600		Manx	Scottish Gaelic		Early Modern Welsh		
1700	Modern Irish				Modern Welsh	Modern Cornish	Modern Breton
1800							
2000							

1.4 Beith-Luis-Fearn: 'Orthodox' Ogham

'Orthodox' Ogham refers to inscriptions in the Archaic Irish period of the language. The original 20 letters are called *feda* (trees / wood), and are arranged into four *aicmí* (classes / families):

The word alphabet comes from the Greek *alpha* + *beta*, the first two letters in the sequence. Likewise, ogham is also referred to as the '*Beith-Luis-Fearn*' or '*Beith-Luis-Nin*'.

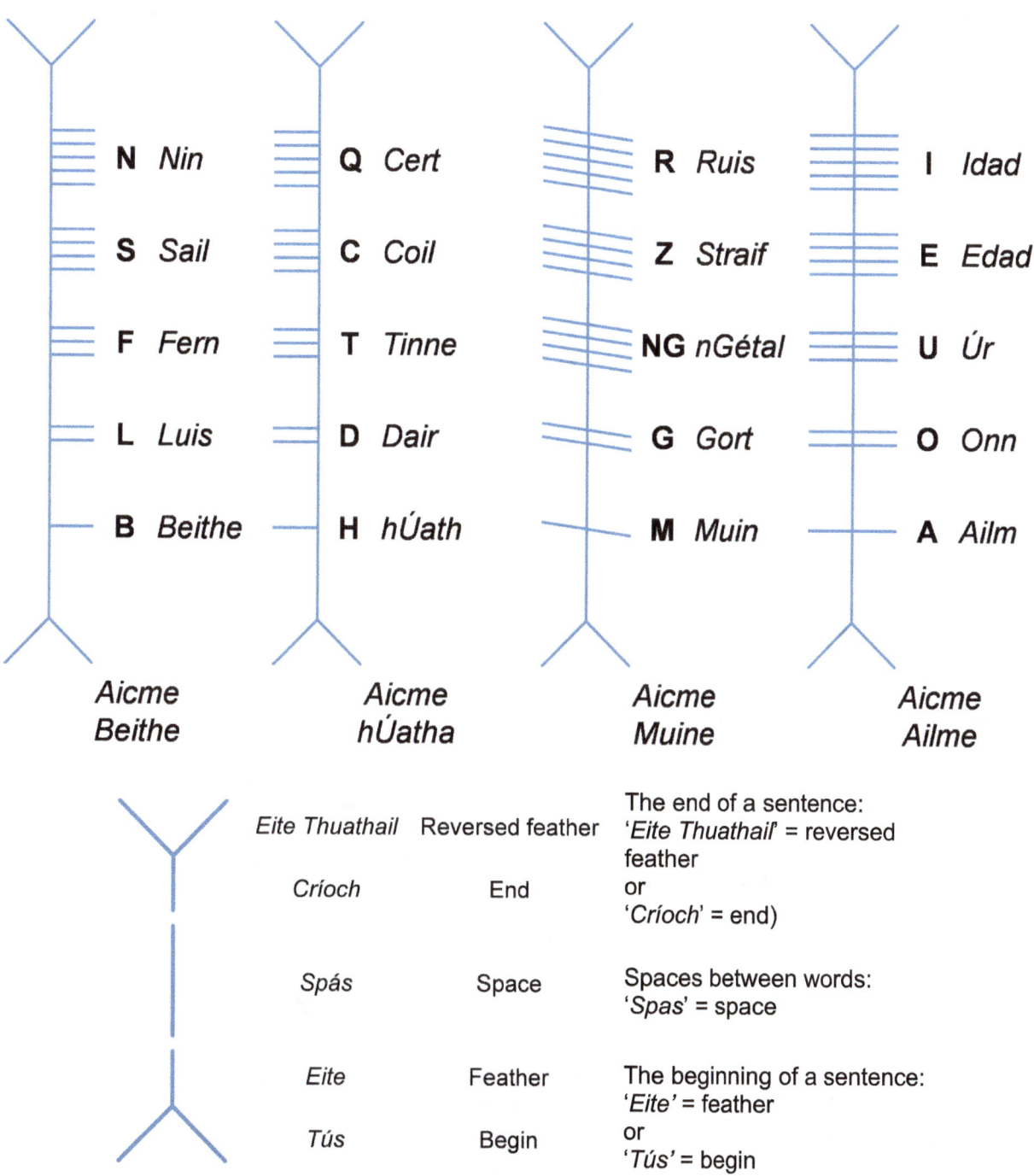

1.5   *Beith-Luis-Fearn*: 'Scholastic' Ogham and the '*Forfeda*'

'Scholastic' Ogham refers to inscriptions and manuscripts in the Old Irish period of the language. They are called 'scholastic' because they are believed to have been inspired by manuscript sources, rather than a continuation of the traditional 'orthodox' carvings, carving the stem of the letter on to the face, instead of using the *droim* or *faobhar* (edge) of the stone.

An additional 6 letters were later added, their group name '*Forfeda*' coming from the words *for* (additional) and *fid* (tree / wood).

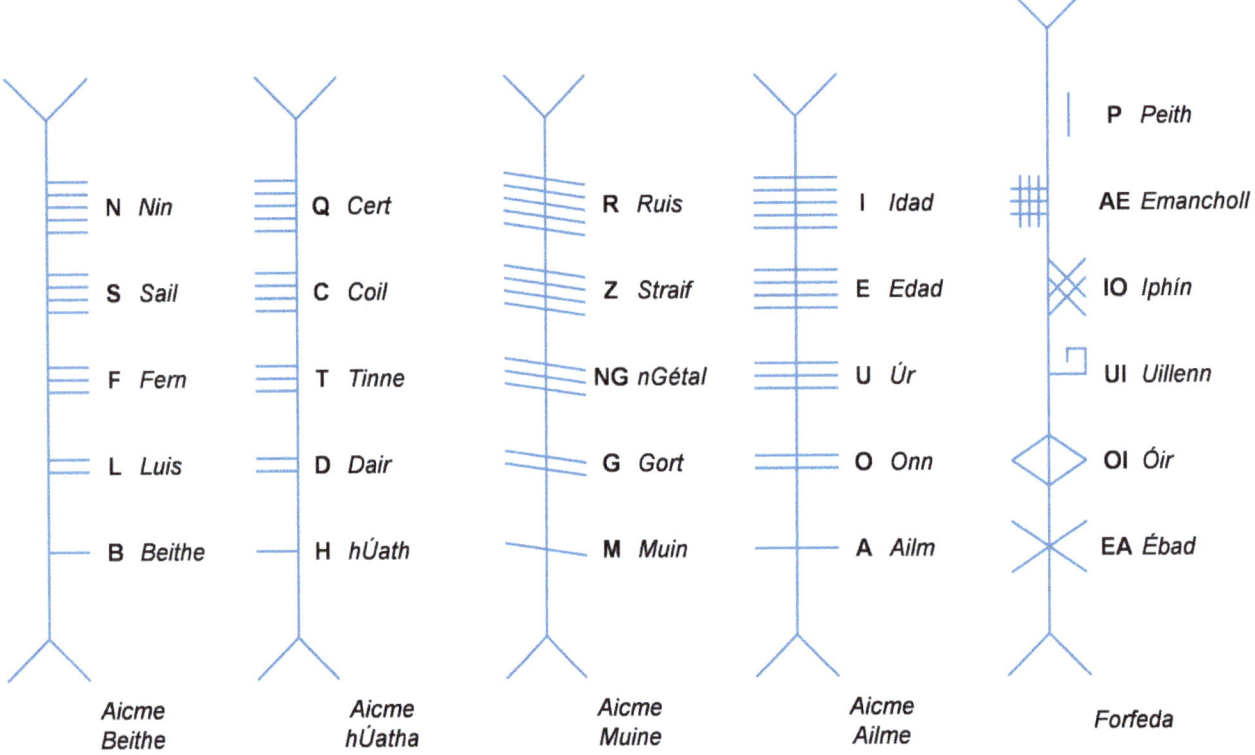

Some letters in the Latin alphabet that we use do not have an equivalent in ogham, but substitutions can be made in transliteration:

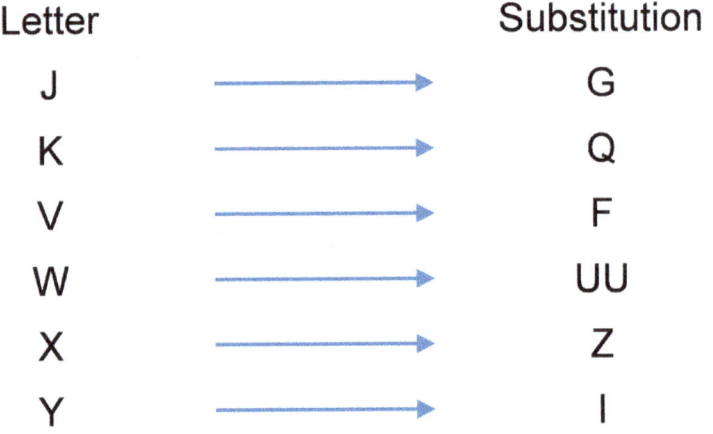

1.6 *Beith-Luis-Fearn*: 'Scholastic' Ogham: Horizontal

Manuscripts began to display ogham in horizontal form, rather than the vertical bottom-to-top format.

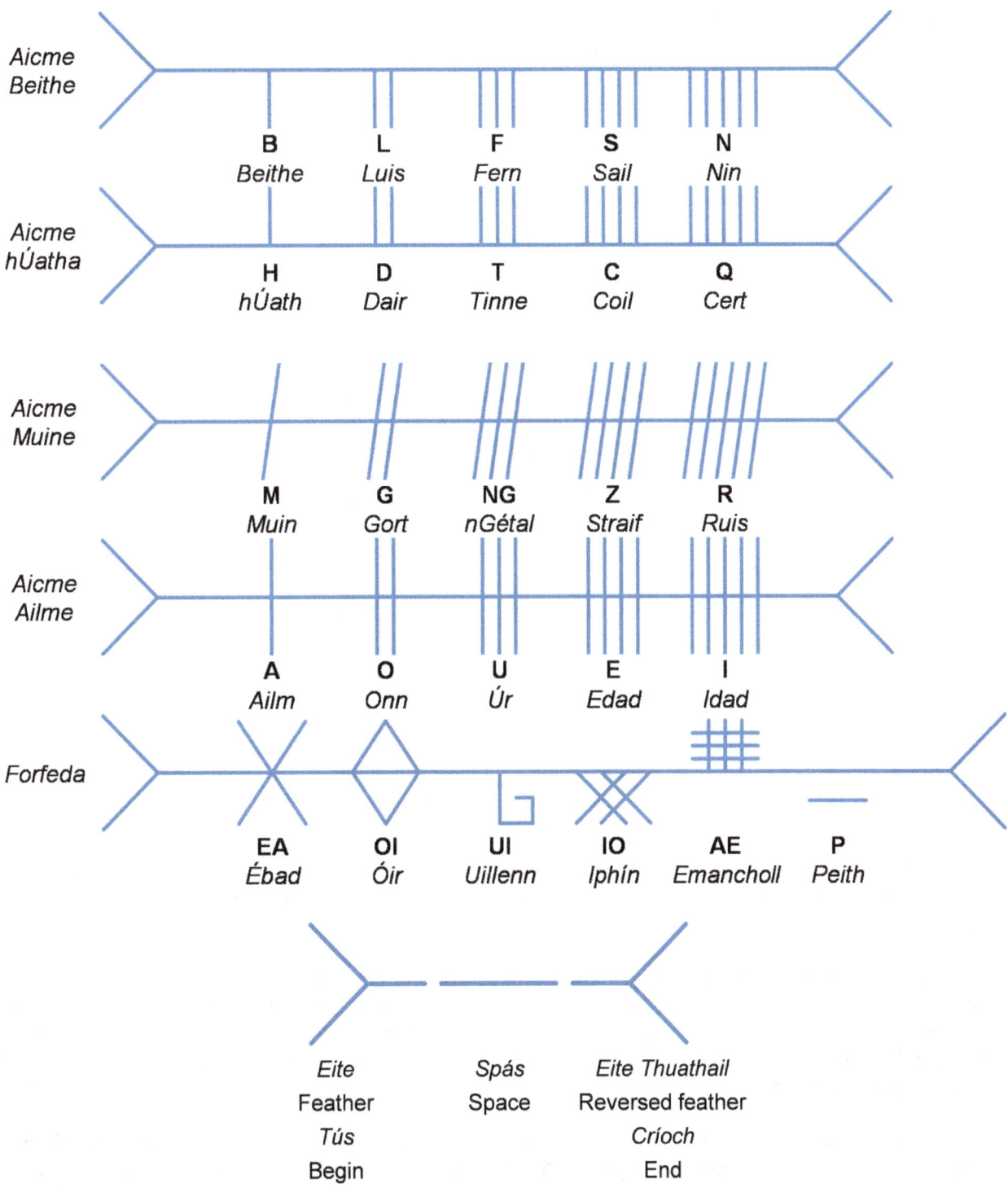

2 The Book of Ballymote

The Book of Ballymote (*Leabhar Bhaile an Mhóta*) was written in around 1390 or 1391 in the town of Ballymote in North West Ireland. It was commissioned by Tonnaltagh McDonagh and compiled by Manus O'Duignan and Solomon O'Droma among others. It is a compilation of older texts, documents and important works handed down from antiquity. Today it is preserved in the Royal Irish Academy (MS 23 P 12).

Of particular interest in the Book of Ballymote are the two works *In Lebor Ogaim* (The Book of Ogams) and *Auraicept na n-Éces* (The Scholar's Primer).

2.1 *In Lebor Ogaim* (The Book of Ogams)

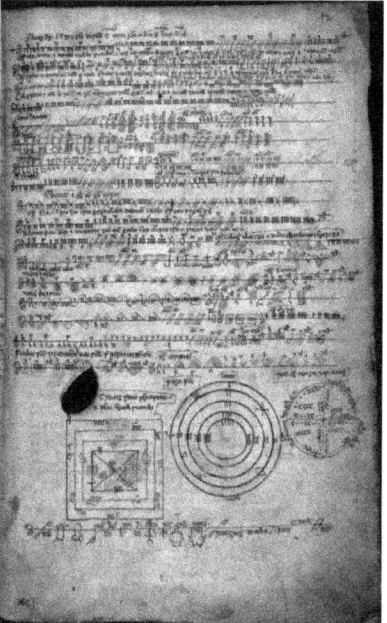

Folio 170v of '*In Lebor Ogaim*'
Source: Wikipedia Creative Commons

In Lebor Ogaim does not have its own title in the manuscript, but it is referred to by the *Auraicept na n-Éces* that follows it in the book as '*as amal isber in leapar ogaim*', which is where the given title of *In Lebor Ogaim* comes from.

At the time this book was written, poets were part of an elite class of people in Ireland and Scotland called *filí* (singular: *file*), and their training would include the learning and memorising of a hundred and fifty different varieties of ogham in the first three years of their study. It is also worth noting that the 'Younger Futhark' of runes are also included as a kind of ogham, described as *ogam lochlannach* (ogham of the Norsemen).

Also known as the 'Ogam Tract', this work lists around a hundred variations of ogham alphabets or 'scales' for use in secret codes, tallying numbers, encoding messages, etc. Some are even thought to have been used to notate music, such as the playing of the Celtic harp, on account of each letter containing up to five stems, representing the thumb and fingers of each hand, however the lack of evidence of exactly how the Celtic harp was played makes it difficult for historians or musicologists to reach any conclusion.

Ogham   2. The Book of Ballymote

Ardach Finn Andso Sis - Ladder of Fionn (01)

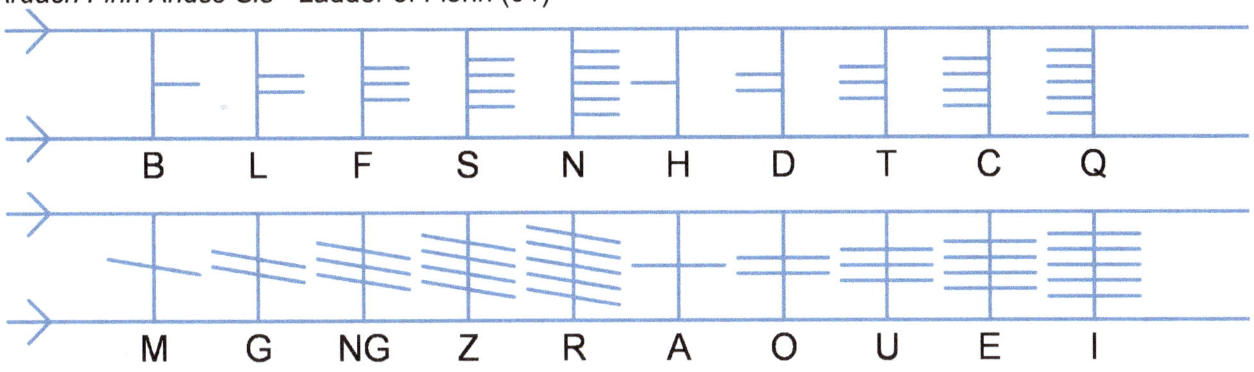

Et Reliqua Sic Foraicme I N-Ar Ndeigh - Another Example (02)

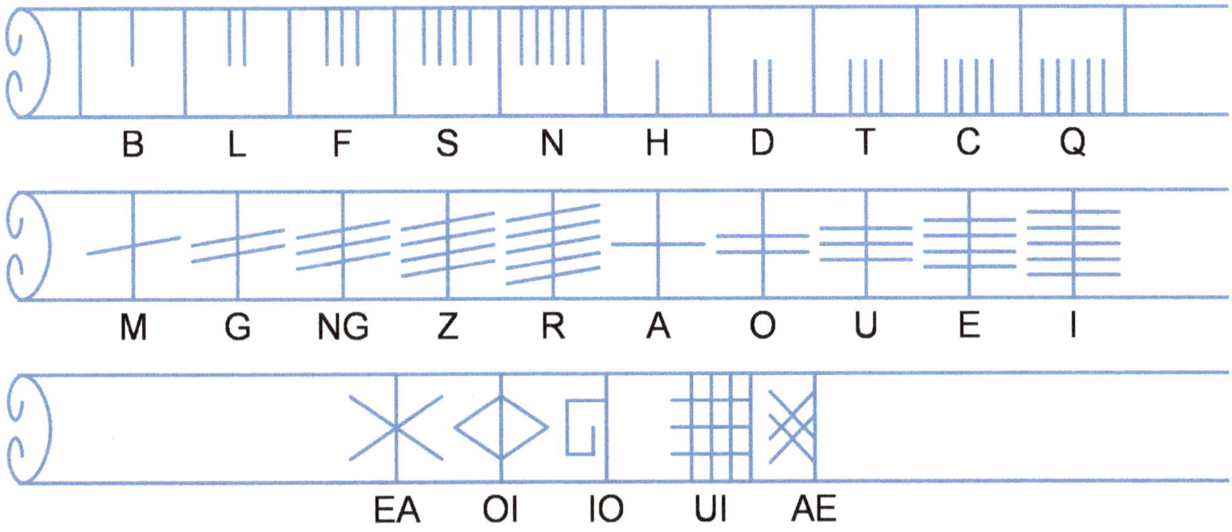

Luthogam Andso - Hinge Ogham (03)

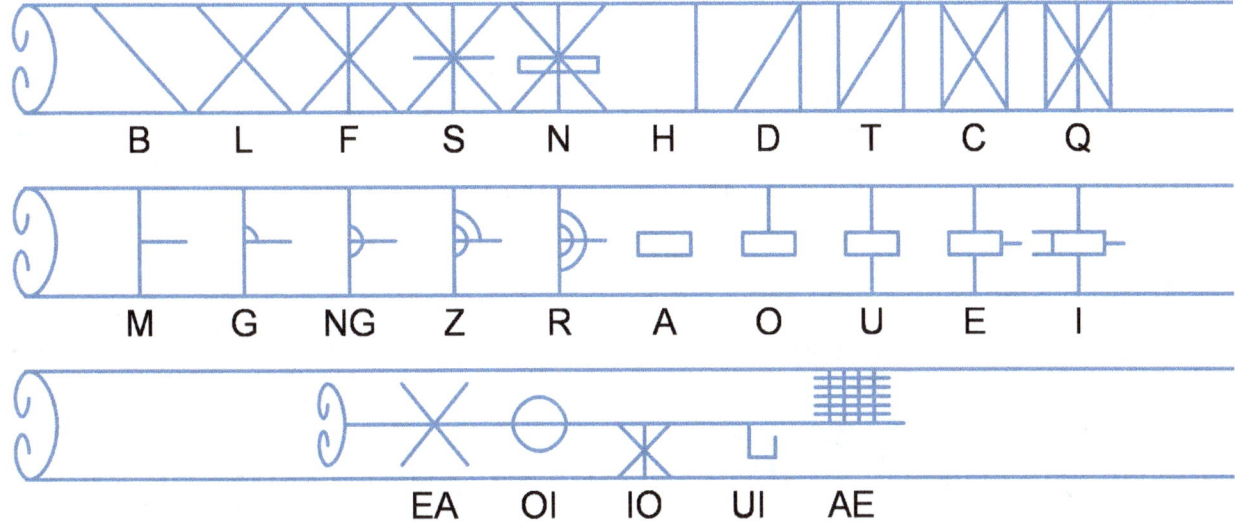

Ogham 2. The Book of Ballymote

Tredruimnech So - Three Stemmed Ogham (04)

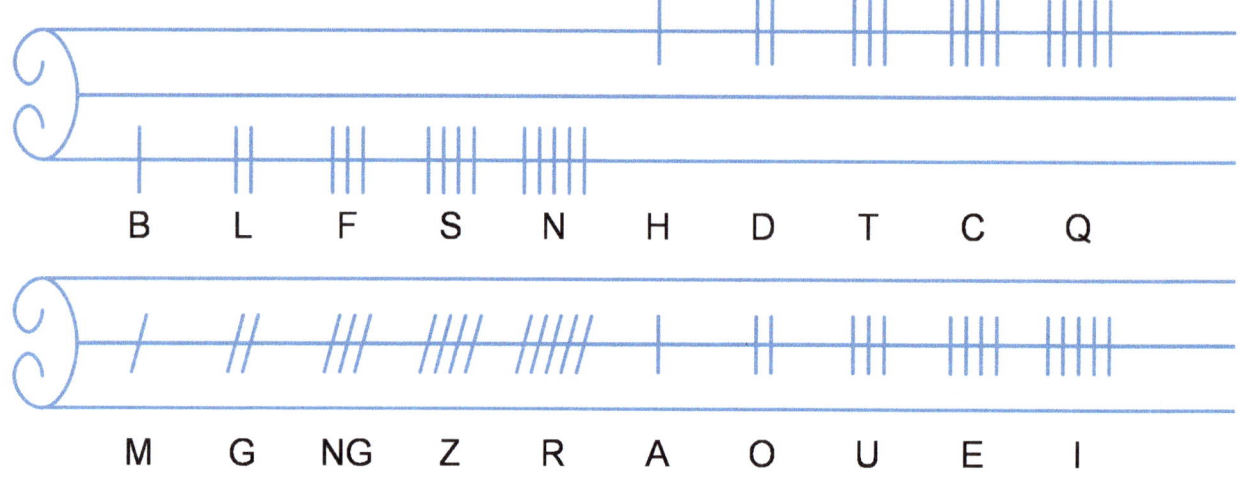

Trelurgach Find - Three Stemmed Ogham of Fionn (05)

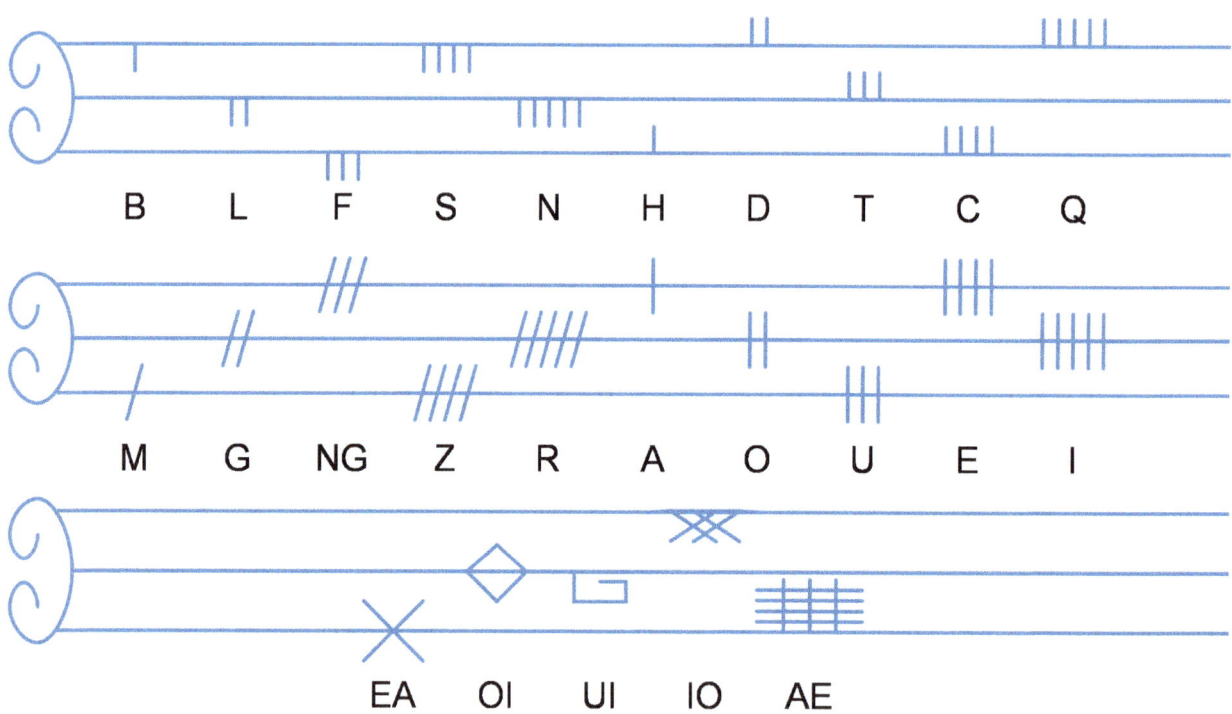

Ladogam - Channel Ogham (06)

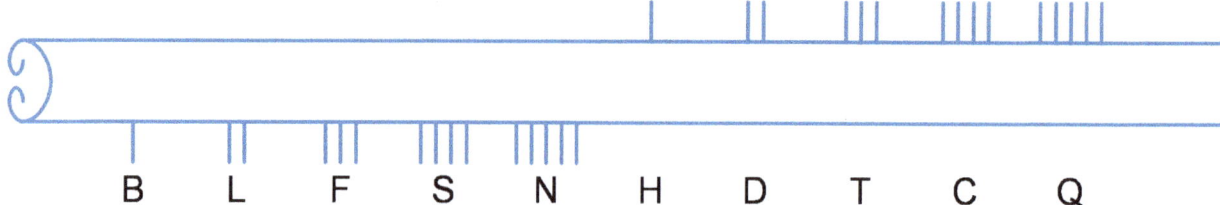

Ogham 2. The Book of Ballymote

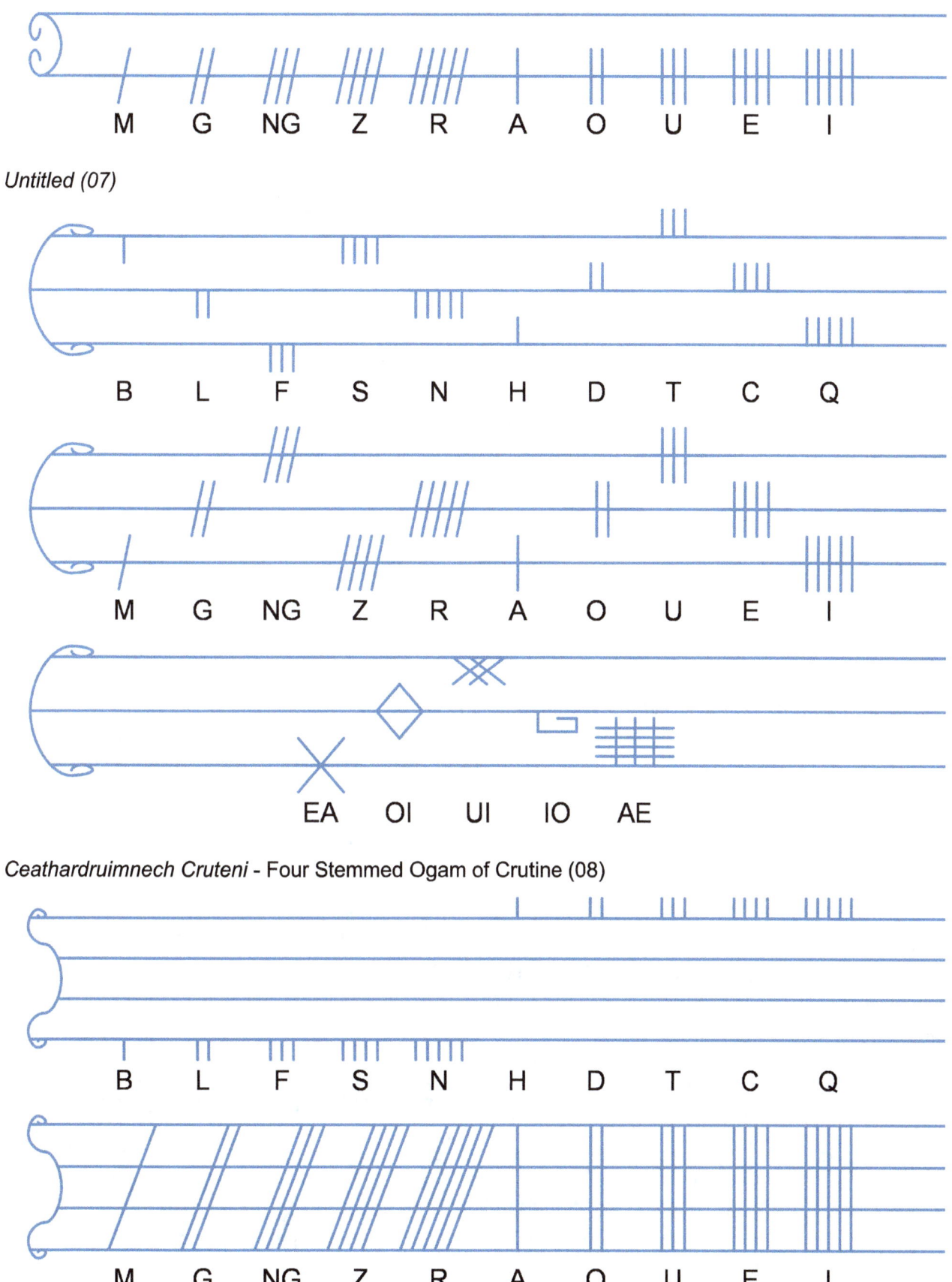

Untitled (07)

Ceathardruimnech Cruteni - Four Stemmed Ogam of Crutine (08)

Ogham
2. The Book of Ballymote

Aliter Bethi, Mar So Uili - A Different Way of Writing (09)

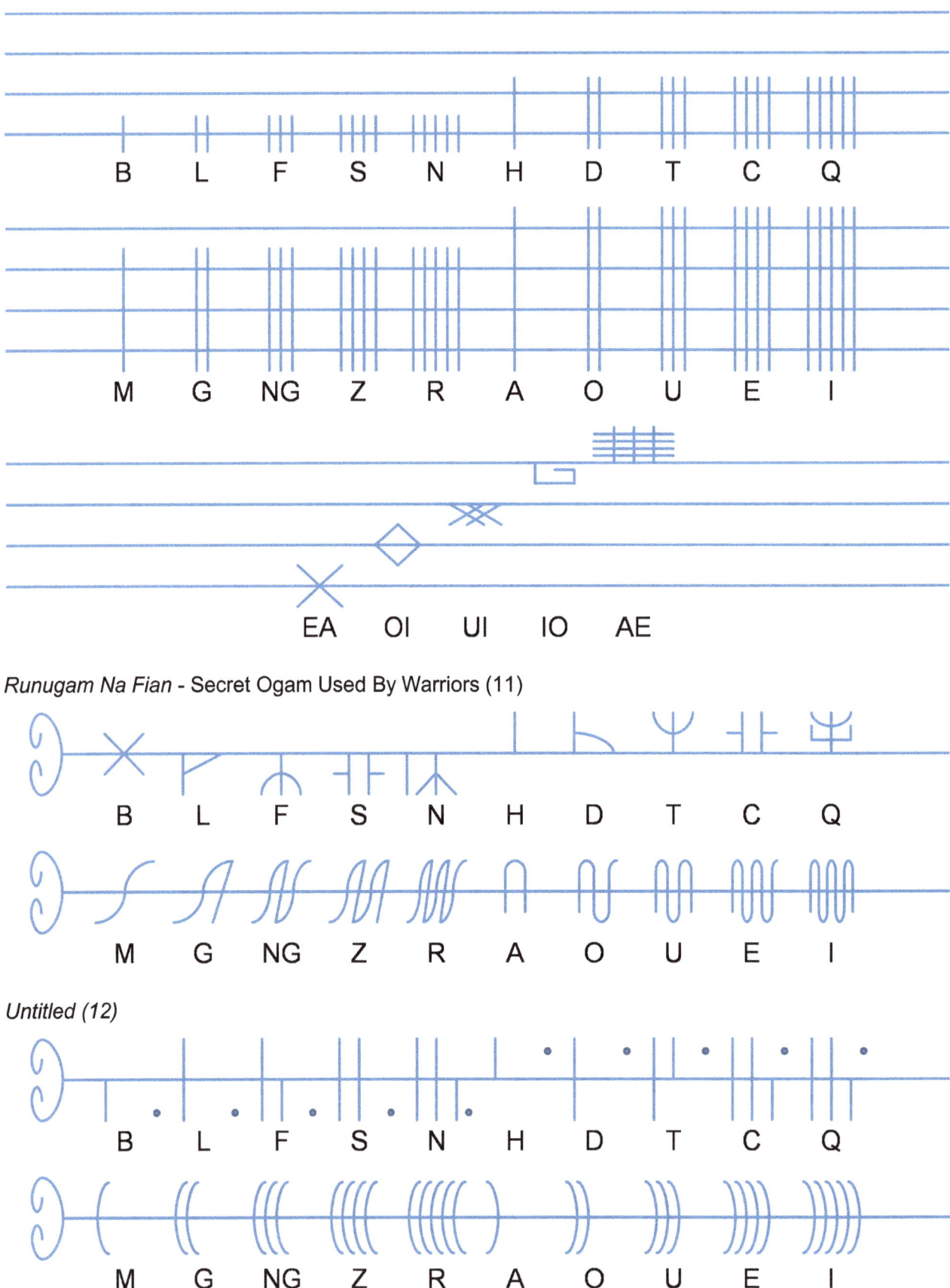

Runugam Na Fian - Secret Ogam Used By Warriors (11)

Untitled (12)

Ogham   *2. The Book of Ballymote*

Ebadach Ilaind - X Shaped Ogham (13)

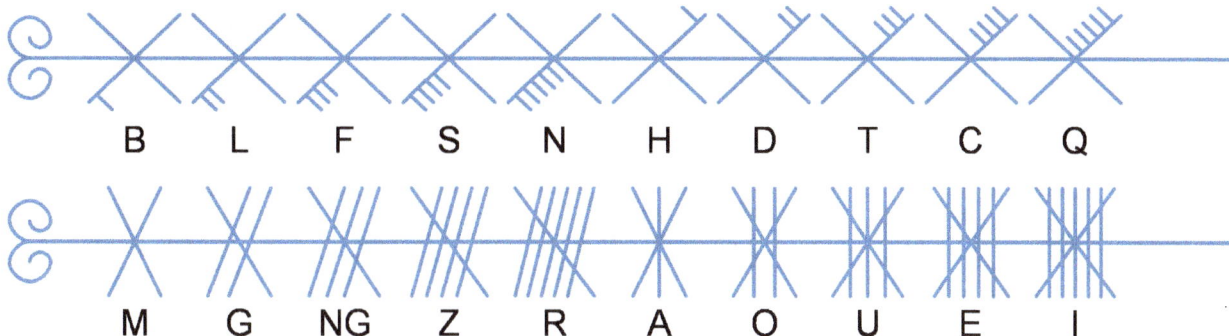

Ogam Briccrenn - Ogam of Bricriu (14)

This alphabet is named after Briciu, who was a satirical poet who served at the court of *Conchubar Mac Neasa* in Ulster. He was well known for his sharp wit, and wicked tongue.

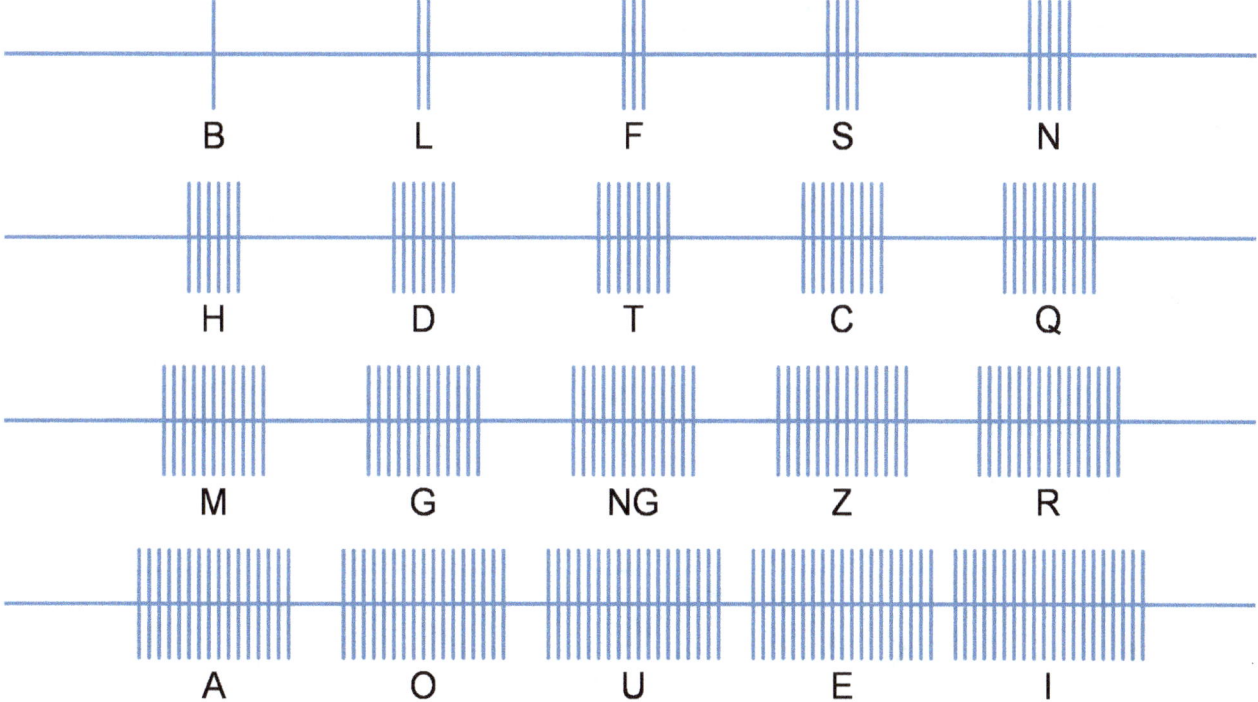

Ogam Adlenfid - Letter Rack Ogham (17)

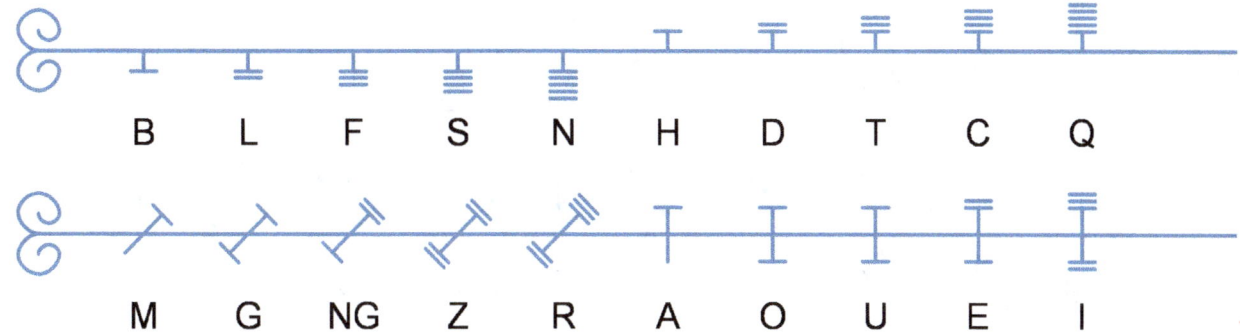

Ogham
2. The Book of Ballymote

Crad Cride Ecis - Anguish of A Poet's Heart (19)

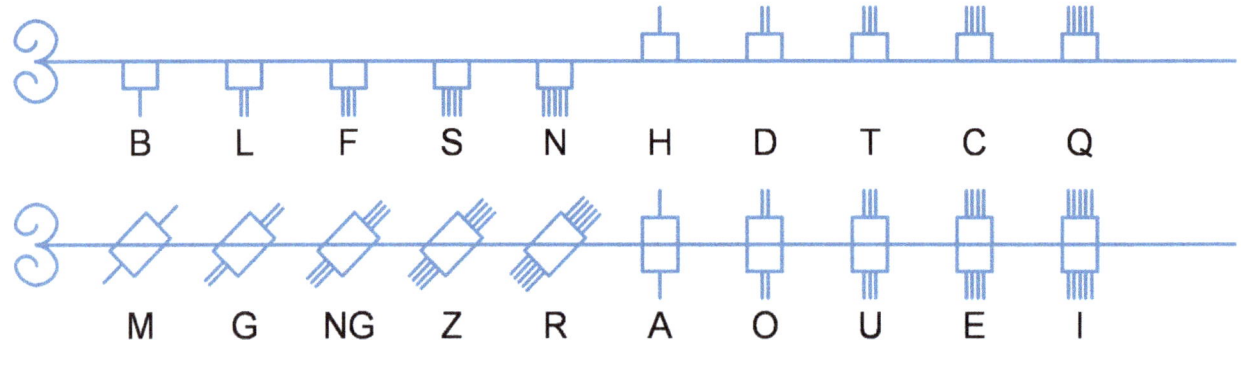

Ogam Rind Fri Derc - Point To Eye Ogham (36)

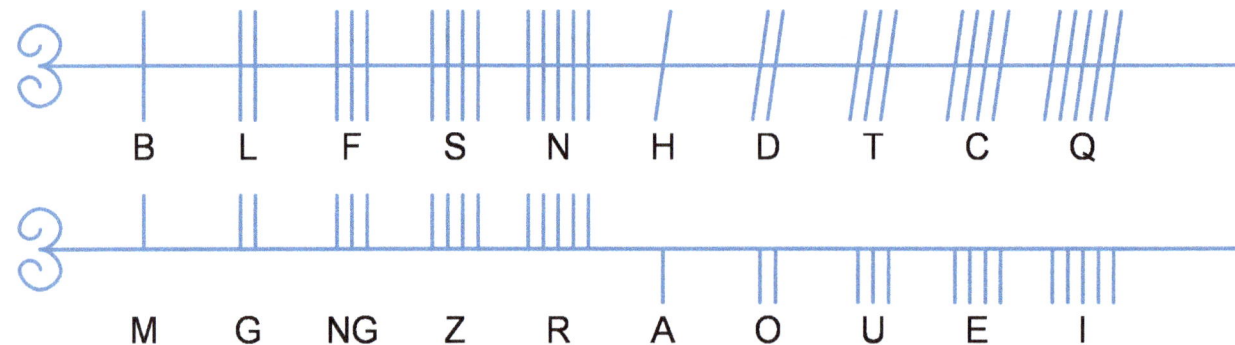

Brec Mor - Great Dotting (40)

Brecor Beo - Lively Dotting (49)

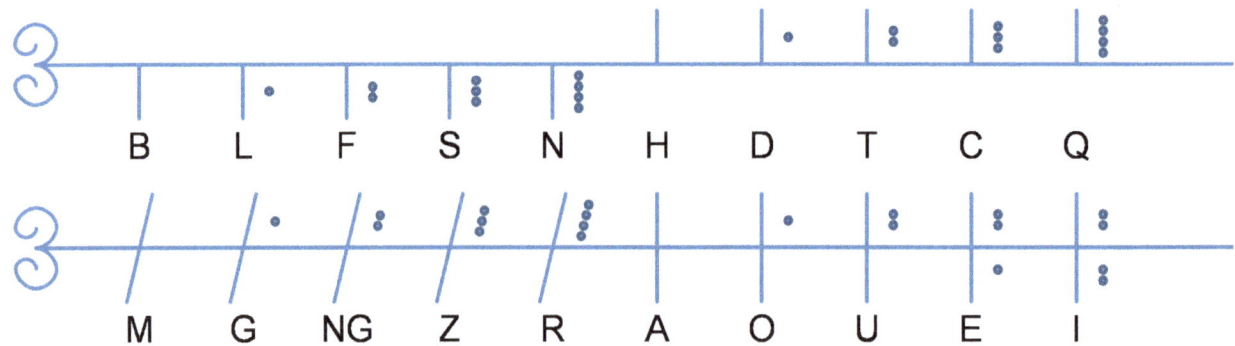

Ogham   2. The Book of Ballymote

Ceand Imreasan - Strife Head (50)

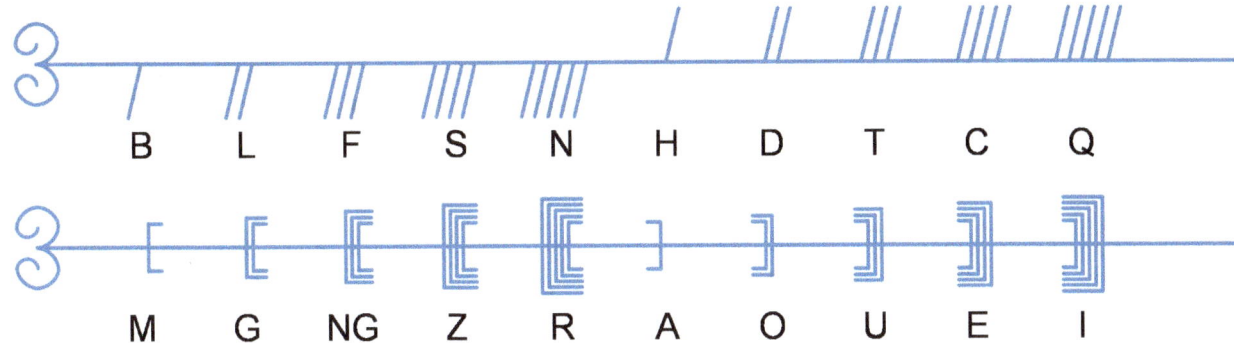

Ogam Dedad - Ogham of Dedu (51)

The Dedu (*Clanna Dedad*) is another name for the *Érainn* or Iverni who Ireland is named after.

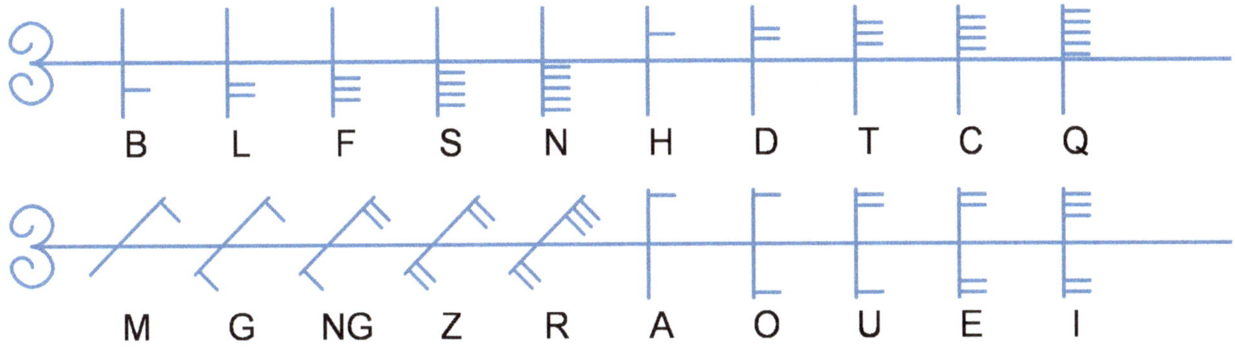

Untitled (53)

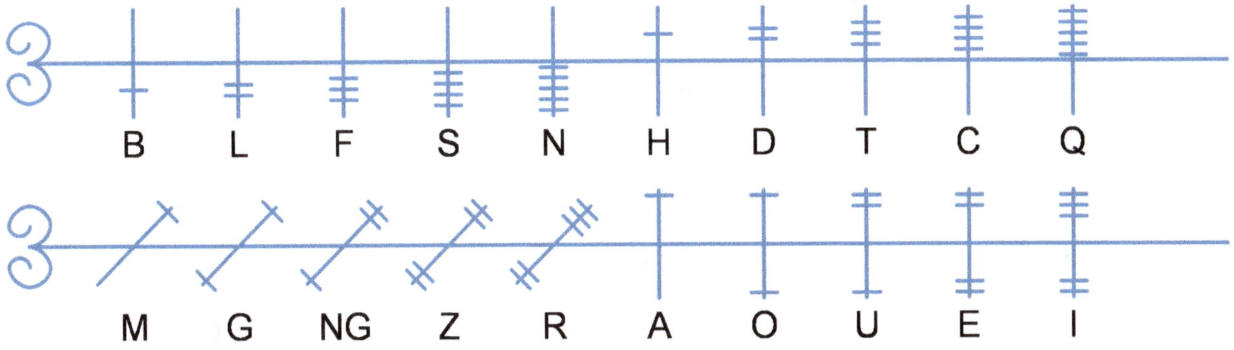

Insnitheach - Infilleted (54)

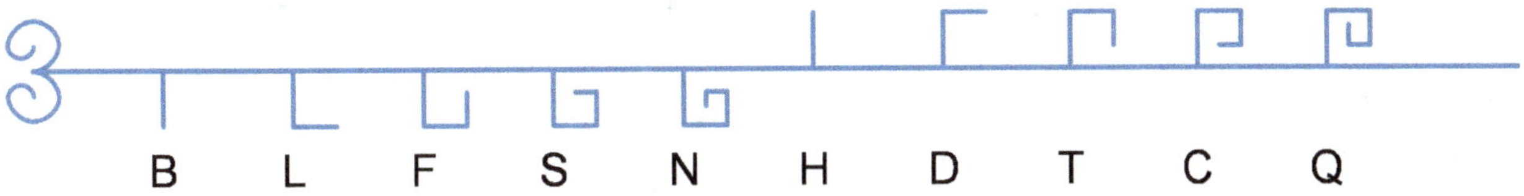

Ogham   2. The Book of Ballymote

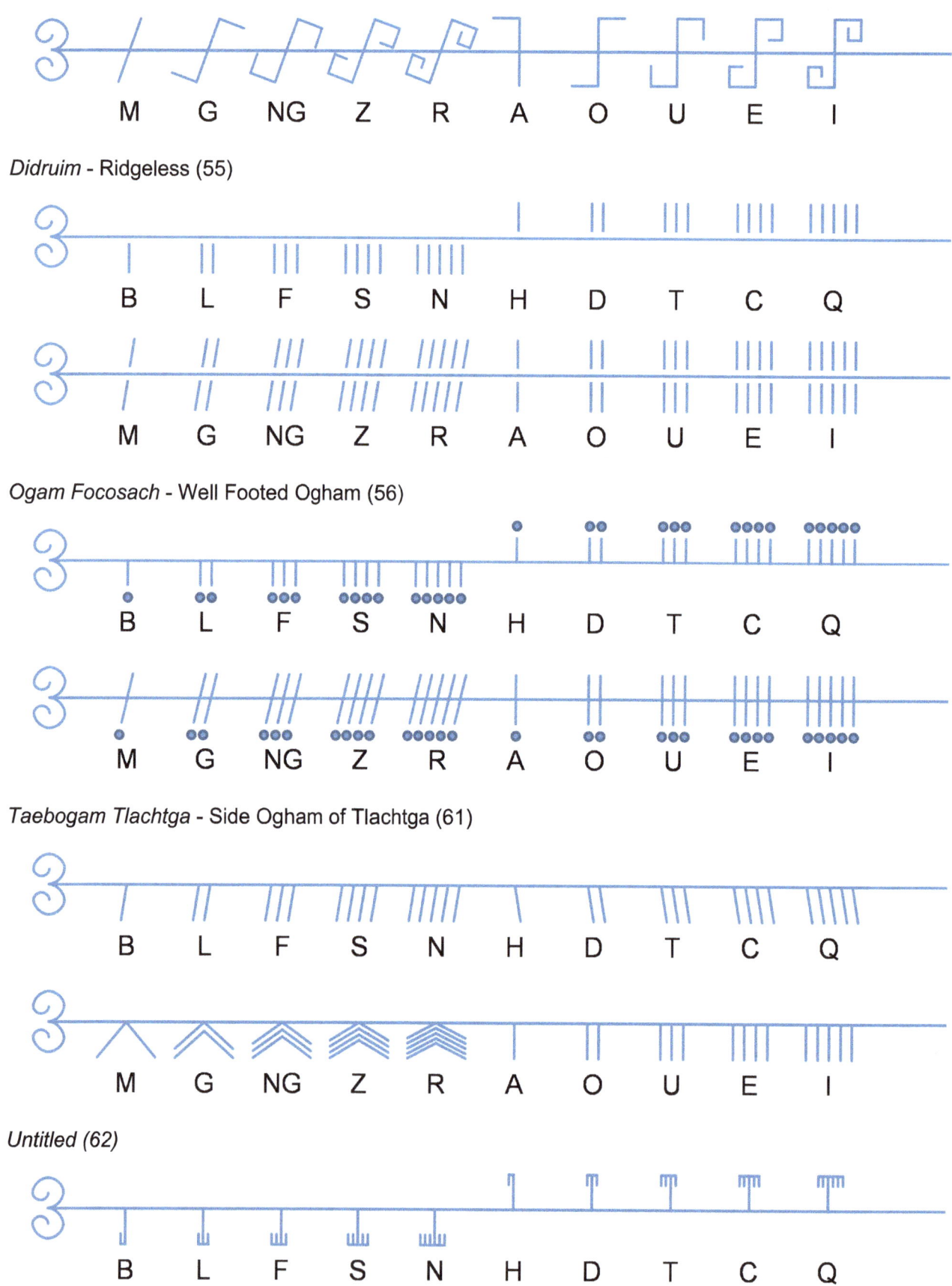

Didruim - Ridgeless (55)

Ogam Focosach - Well Footed Ogham (56)

Taebogam Tlachtga - Side Ogham of Tlachtga (61)

Untitled (62)

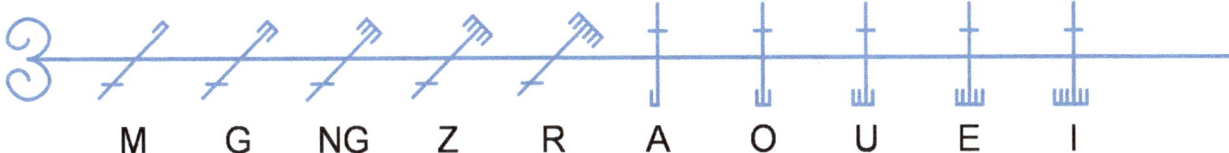

Ogam Erimoin - Ogham of Erimon (63)

This variety is named after Erimon, the son of Mil, the leader of the Milesians, the last of the peoples to settle in Ireland after sailing from Iberia (Hispania) after spending thousands of years travelling the earth.

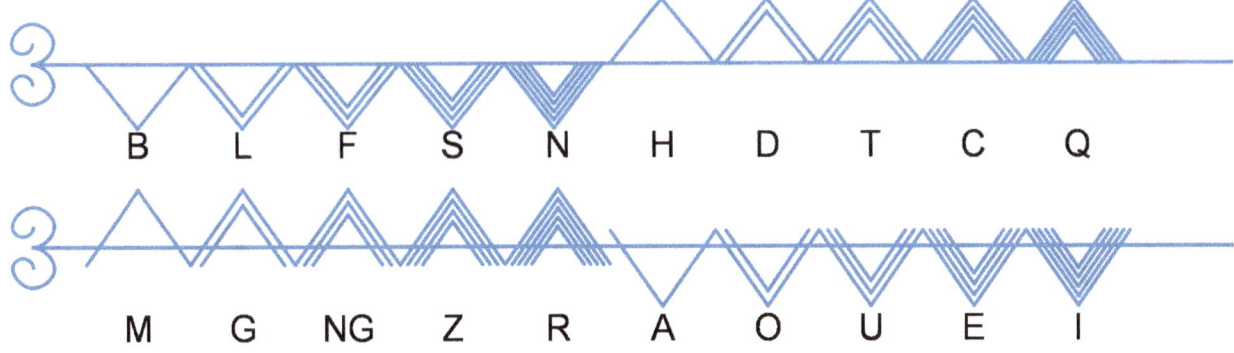

Snalthi Snimach - Interwoven Thread (64)

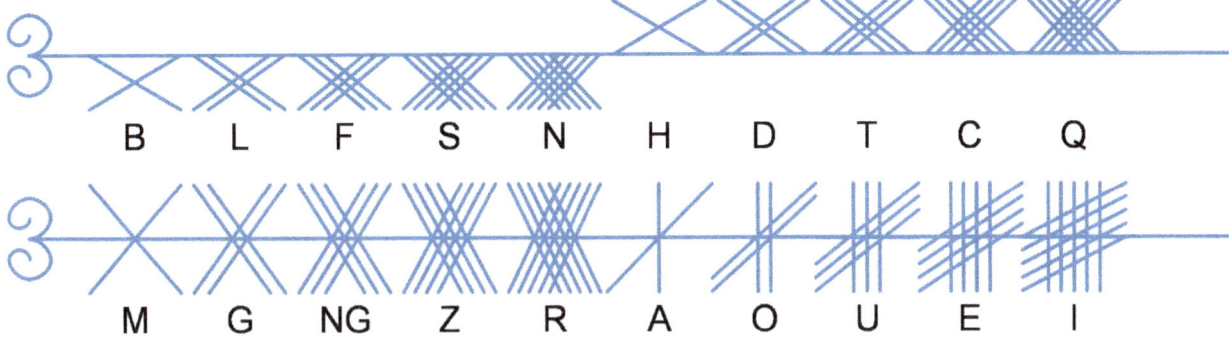

Ogam Alrenach - Shield Ogham (73)

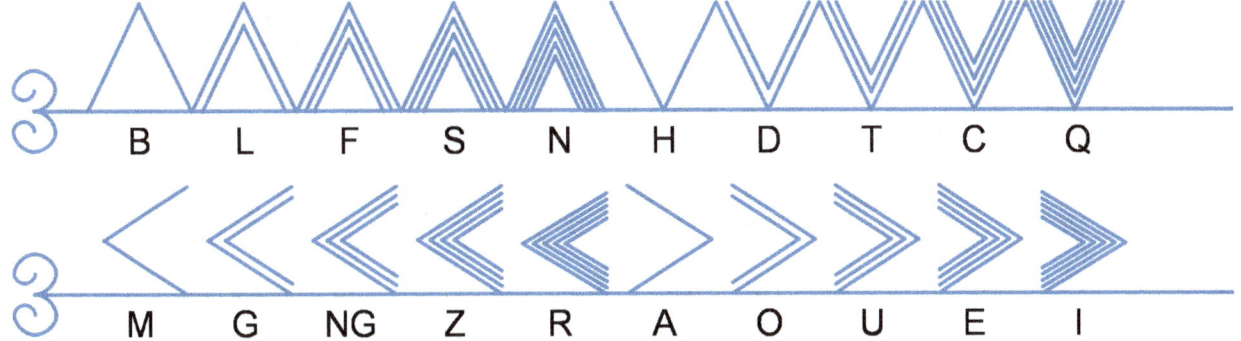

Fege Find - Fionn's Window (75)

The word *'fege'* also means a ridge-pole used to hold up a house. It is thought that this variety is meant to depict or invoke an image of a circular Iron Age house. It is named after Fionn mac Cumhaill, a great warrior and mythical hunter of Irish mythology. The stories of Fionn form *an Fhiannaíocht* (The Feenian Cycle), much of which is told from the perspective of Fionn's son *Oisín* (Ossian). One theory is that this pattern was used on a casting cloth, where ogham sticks would be cast on to the cloth, and then interpreted according to where the sticks landed in relation to the pattern and each other.

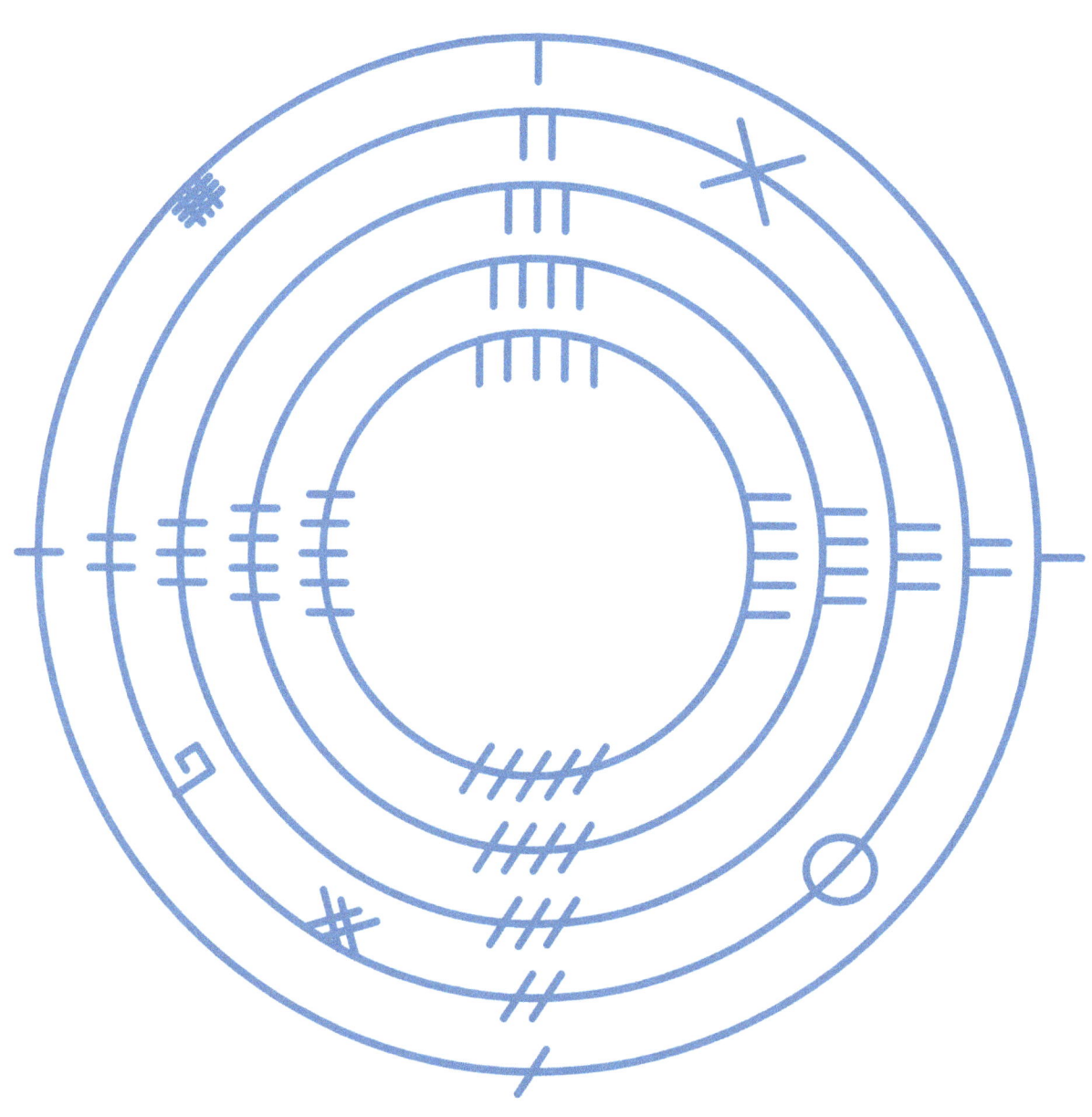

Ogham 2. The Book of Ballymote

Untitled (Sacred Branch Ogham) (89)

This variety although originally untitled was later referred to as 'Sacred Branch Ogham', on account of its resemblance to trees. It is believed to have been one of the varieties designed and developed to be used for divination and other magical and ritual purposes.

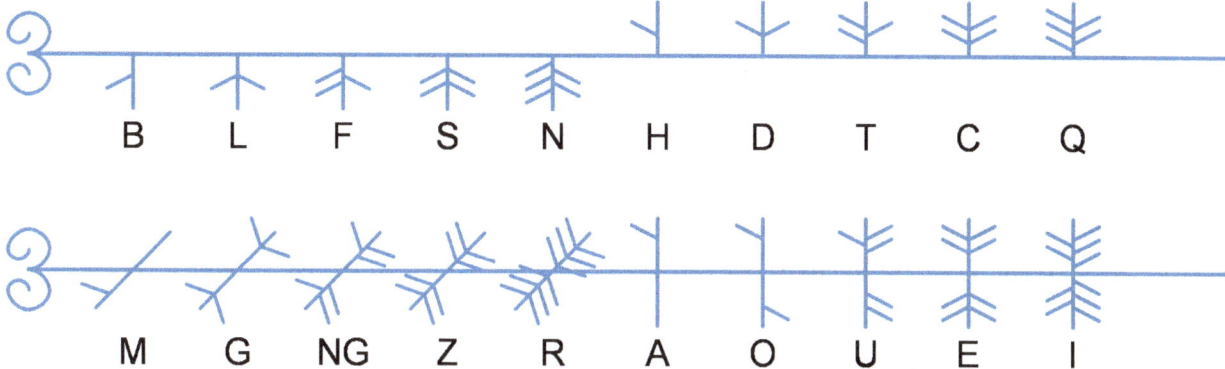

The forms of the letters and the sequential accumulation of branches in each *aicme* has undergone some minor changes since, perhaps to better facilitate their use when carved on to stones or twigs, so that regardless of which way up they land when cast, it is still easy to distinguish each letter.

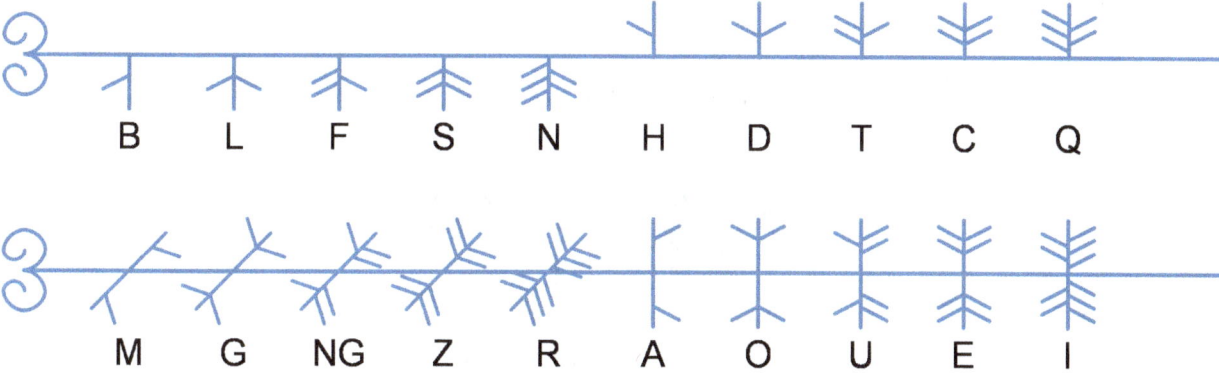

2.2 *Auraicept na n-Éces* (The Scholar's Primer)

The *Auraicept na n-Éces*, is believed to date back to a 7th century core text written by a scholar named Longarad. Subsequent additions were made before the production of the earliest surviving copy in the 12th century. It contains the origin of the idea that the Ogham letters are named after and represent trees. As well as the 'Book of Ballymote', this work is also preserved in:

- The 'Book of Leinster' (Trinity College Dublin H. 2. 18., c1160)
- The 'Yellow Book of Lecan' (Trinity College Dublin, H. 2. 16., c1391-1401)
- The 'Edgerton' Manuscript no. 88 (British Library, 1564)

"This is their number: five Oghmic groups, i.e., five men for each group, and one up to five for each of them, that their signs may be distinguished.

These are their signs: right of stem, left of stem, athwart of stem, through stem, about stem.

Thus is a tree climbed, to wit, treading on the root of the tree first with thy right hand first and thy left hand after.

Then with the stem, and against it and through it and about it".[1]

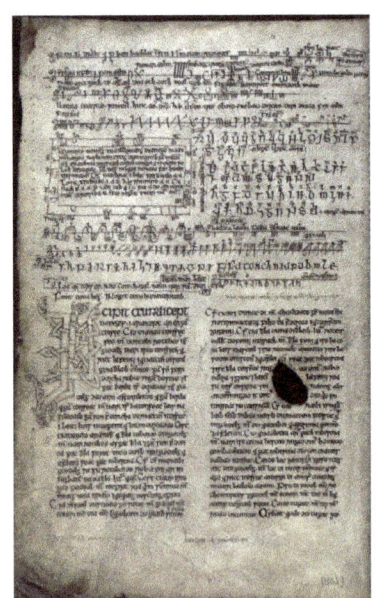

Folio 170r of *'Auraicept na n-Éces'*
Source: Wikipedia Creative Commons

---

[1] Calder, George *'Auraicept na N-Éces*, The Scholar's Primer', John Grant, Edinburgh, 1917

3 *Bríatharogaim*: Meanings

The meanings of the names of the ogham letters are described using kennings. A kenning is a literary or poetic device used by the writer or poet to talk around or hint at a specific word or term. This figure of speech is usually in the form of a compound of two or more words acting as a figurative metaphor.

The list of meanings is called the *Bríatharogam* (word-ogham), the plural is *Bríatharogaim*, and there are three different versions:

    A. *Bríatharogam Morainn mac Moín*
    B. *Bríatharogam Maic ind Óc*
    C. *Bríatharogam Con Culainn*

No.		Letter	Name	Meaning	*Bríatharogaim*	
1		B	BEITHE BEITH	Birch tree	A. B. C.	*féochos foltchain* ('withered foot with fine hair') *glaisem cnis* ('greyest of skin') *maise malach* ('beauty of the eyebrow')
2		L	LUIS LUIS	Blaze, plant, or herb	A. B. C.	*lí súla* ('lustre of the eye') *carae cethrae* ('friend of cattle') *lúth cethrae* ('sustenance of cattle')
3		F	FERN FEARN	Alder tree	A. B. C.	*airenach fían* ('vanguard of warriors') *comét lachta* ('milk container') *dín cridi* ('protection of the heart')
4		S	SAIL SAIL	Willow tree	A. B. C.	*lí ambi* ('pallor of a lifeless one') *lúth bech* ('sustenance of bees') *tosach mela* ('beginning of honey')
5		N	NIN NION	Fork or loft	A. B. C.	*costud síde* ('establishing of peace') *bág ban* ('boast of women') *bág maise* ('boast of beauty')
6		H	hUATH UATH	Horror or fear	A. B. C.	*condál cúan* ('assembly of packs of hounds') *bánad gnúise* ('blanching of faces') *ansam aidche* ('most difficult at night')
7		D	DAIR DAIR	Oak tree	A. B. C.	*ardam dosae* ('highest tree') *grés soír* ('handicraft of a craftsman') *slechtam soíre* ('most carved of craftsmanship')

Ogham   3. *Bríatharogaim: Meanings*

No.		Letter	Name	Meaning	Bríatharogaim
8		T	*TINNE* *TINNE*	Bar of metal or ingot	A. *trian roith* ('one of three parts of a wheel') B. *smiur gúaile* ('marrow of (char)coal') C. *trian n-airm* ('one of three parts of a weapon')
9		C	*COLL* *COLL*	Hazel tree	A. *caíniu fedaib* ('fairest tree') B. *carae blóesc* ('friend of nutshells') C. *milsem fedo* ('sweetest tree')
10		Q	*CERT* *CEIRT*	Bush, oak, rag, or apple	A. *clithar baiscill* ('shelter of a [lunatic?]') B. *bríg anduini* ('substance of an insignificant person') C. *dígu fethail* ('dregs of clothing')
11		M	*MUIN* *MUIN*	Neck, throat, upper back, wile, ruse, love, esteem	A. *tressam fedmae* ('strongest in exertion') B. *árusc n-airlig* ('proverb of slaughter') C. *conar gotha* ('path of the voice')
12		G	*GORT* *GORT*	Field	A. *milsiu féraib* ('sweetest grass') B. *ined erc* ('suitable place for cows') C. *sásad ile* ('sating of multitudes')
13		NG	*nGÉTAL* *NGÉADAL*	Killing, slays	A. *lúth lego* ('sustenance of a leech') B. *étiud midach* ('raiment of physicians') C. *tosach n-échto* ('beginning of slaying')
14		Z	*STRAIPH* *STRAIF*	Sulphur	A. *tressam rúamnai* ('strongest reddening (dye)') B. *mórad rún* ('increase of secrets') C. *saigid nél* ('seeking of clouds')
15		R	*RUIS* *RUIS*	Red or redness	A. *tindem rucci* ('most intense blushing') B. *rúamnae drech* ('reddening of faces') C. *bruth fergae* ('glow of anger')
16		A	*AILM* *AILM*	Pine tree	A. *ardam íachta* ('loudest groan') B. *tosach frecrai* ('beginning of an answer') C. *tosach garmae* ('beginning of calling')

No.		Letter	Name	Meaning	Bríatharogaim
17		O	ONN ONN	Ash tree	A. *congnaid ech* ('wounder of horses') B. *féthem soíre* ('smoothest of craftsmanship') C. *lúth fían* ('[equipment] of warrior bands')
18		U	ÚR ÚR	Earth, clay, soil, heath	A. *úaraib adbaib* ('in cold dwellings') B. *sílad cland* ('propagation of plants') C. *forbbaid ambí* ('shroud of a lifeless one')
19		E	EDAD EADHADH	Test tree, aspen tree	A. *érgnaid fid* ('discerning tree') B. *commaín carat* ('exchange of friends') C. *bráthair bethi* ('brother of birch')
20		I	IDAD IODHADH	Yew tree	A. *sinem fedo* ('oldest tree') B. *caínem sen* ('fairest of the ancients') C. *lúth lobair* ('energy of an infirm person')
21		EA	EBHADH EABHADH	Aspen tree	A. *snámchaín feda* ('fair-swimming letter') B. *cosc lobair* ('[admonishing?] of an infirm person') C. *caínem éco* ('fairest fish')
22		OI	ÓR ÓR	Gold	A. *sruithem aicde* ('most venerable substance') B. *lí crotha* ('splendour of form')
23		UI	UILLEAND UILLEANN	Elbow	A. *túthmar fid* ('fragrant tree') B. *cubat oll* ('great elbow / cubit')
24		P IO	IPHIN PÍN IFÍN	Gooseberry or thorn plant	A. *milsem fedo* ('sweetest tree') B. *amram mlais* ('most wonderful taste')
25		X Ch AE	EAMHANCHOLL EAMHANCHOLL	Twin of hazel	A. *lúad sáethaig* ('groan of a sick person') B. *mol galraig* ('groan of a sick person')
26		P	PEITH	Birch tree	The letter P does not appear in Irish until the early Middle Irish period when it was adopted from Latin. It is added here perhaps to distinguish Latin loan words and to distinguish the minimal pair /b/ and /p/.

4 Mythology

4.1 *Lebor Gabála Érenn*: The Book of the Taking of Ireland

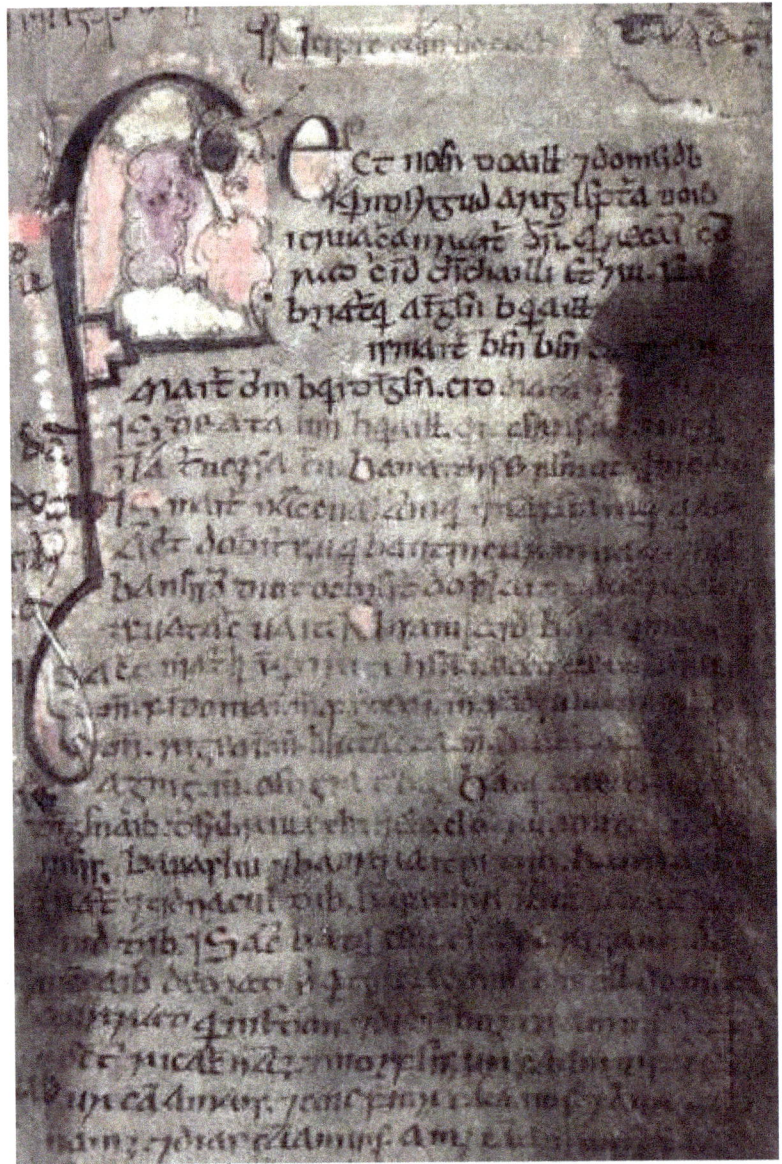

'*Lebor Gabála Érenn*' from Folio 53 of the 'Book of Leinster'
(Trinity College Dublin H. 2. 18., c1160)
Source: Wikipedia Creative Commons

Also called The Book of the Taking of Ireland, The Book of Invasions, or The Book of Conquests, the *Lebor Gabála Érenn* is a collection of poetry and prose telling the history of Ireland and the Irish people from the creation of the world up until the Middle Ages.

The earliest version of this collection is believed to have been compiled by an anonymous writer in the 11th century. Preserved in 19 extant manuscripts, it was translated into English by R. A. S. Macalister between 1937 and 1942. The poetry and prose tells the story of Ireland being settled by six different groups of people:

The Cessairians

Cessair is the daughter of Bith and the granddaughter of Noah. She is not permitted to enter Noah's Ark, and leaves 40 days before the flood arrives. She sets out with her people in three ships, but two of the ships are lost. Those that arrive at *Dun na mBarc* in the south of Ireland are Cessair, 49 other women, and three men, one of whom is her husband Fintan Mac Bochra. The plan is for the three men to divide the women between them, divide Ireland into three, and populate the island, but two of the men die. When the 50 women turn their attention to Fintan, he feels under immense pressure and responsibility, and he turns himself into a salmon and escapes from Ireland. Cessair is heartbroken, and without any men on the island, their plans fail and they perish.

The Partholónians

Partholón is the son of Sera, son of Sru, who is a descendant of Magog, son of Japheth, who is the son of Noah. He sails with his people to Ireland via Sicily and Iberia and arrives at *Inber Scéne* in the south of Ireland roughly 300 to 312 years after the flood. Partholón and all of his people, five thousand men, and four thousand women, die of the plague in a single week.

The Nemedians

Nemed and his people arrive in Ireland 30 years after the plague that kills the people of Partholón. He eventually dies of the plague, and his people are oppressed by the Fomorians, a supernatural race of giants who represent harmful or destructive powers of nature (similar to the Jötnar in Norse Mythology). They rise up against the Fomorians, but most are killed, and the survivors leave Ireland. Some of them flee to Britain, some of them to the north of the world, and some to Greece.

The *Fir Bolg*

The Nemedians who fled from Ireland to Greece become the *Fir Bolg*. They divide Ireland into provinces and rule it for some time before they are overthrown by the *Tuatha Dé Danann*.

The *Tuatha Dé Danann*

The Nemedians who fled from Ireland to the north of the world become the *Tuatha Dé Danann* (People of the goddess of Danu). They are also known as *Tuath Dé* (The Tribe of The Gods). They travel from four cities to Ireland and are said to arrive in dark clouds, as they burn their boats on arrival, bringing darkness for three days and three nights. From each of the cities they have brought four magical treasures with them, Dadga's Cauldron, The Spear of Lugh, *Lia Fáil* (The Stone of Fal), and *Claíomh Solais* (the Sword of Light). They battle and overthrow the *Fir Bolg*. They are seen as gods by the pagan Irish, and fairies by the later Christians.

The Milesians

The Milesians (Irish: *gairthear Mílidh Easpáinne*, Latin: Miles Hispaniaie = soldiers of Hispania) represent the modern day Irish people. They are Gaels who sail from Iberia (Hispania) to Ireland after spending hundreds of years travelling the earth. They agree with the *Tuatha Dé Danann* to divide Ireland between them. The Milesians take the world above, and the *Tuatha Dé Danann* take the world below, i.e. the Otherworld.

A depiction of the *Tuatha Dé Danann* in 'Riders of the Sidhe' by John Duncan, 1911
Source: Wikipedia Creative Commons

4.2 '*Ogma*': The Father of Ogham

Source: Wikipedia Creative Commons

According to the *In Lebor Ogaim* (The Ogham Tract), '*Ogma*' is a member of the *Tuatha Dé Danann*, skilled in speech and poetry. To prove his ingenuity, he invents a way of transcribing speech, and transmits languages and poetry to humans using rays of light.

He is described as the father of Ogham, and his hand is its mother.

The name '*Ogma*' is believed to originate from the Indo European root *ak-* or *ag-* meaning to cut, referring to the method with which ogham was carved into stone and wood.

He is also referred to as *Grianainech*, meaning 'sun-faced' or *Trenfher*, meaning 'strongman', possibly equivalent to the god '*Ogmios*' in Gaul, Celtic France.

This depiction of '*Ogma*' is a bronze figure sculpted by artist Lee Lawrie in 1939, and is a door detail situated in the east entrance of the Library of Congress in Washington D.C.

4.3 Auraicept na n-Éces (The Scholar's Primer)

The *Auraicept na n-Éces* contains several stories about the origins of the Irish people, language, and the Ogham alphabet.

The Book of Fénius Farsaidh

Fénius Farsaidh, the legendary king of Scythia, a region of Central Eurasia in classical antiquity, travels from Scythia with a large group of scholars to study the languages that are being spoken around the biblical Tower of Babel, only to find the people have all dispersed. Fénius sends his scholars to find them and study their language, using the tower as a base.

After ten years the scholars return, and Fénius creates *in Bérla tóbaide* (the selected language) taking the best of all the other languages, and inventing the '*Beithe-Luis-Nuin*' as a writing system, and after having discovered the Hebrew, Greek, and Latin alphabets, the Ogham was considered the most perfected because it was discovered last.

The Book of Amergin

Amergin Glúingel is a bard, a druid, and a judge for the Milesians in Irish Mythology. He was appointed as chief '*Ollam*' (poet or bard) in Ireland by his two brothers who were kings.

He took part in the Milesian conquest of Ireland from the *Tuatha Dé Danann*, firstly as an impartial judge to decide the rules of battle between the two parties, and then by assisting the Milesians in reaching the shore to attack by singing an invocation calling upon the spirit of Ireland, which is known as 'The Song of Amergin'.

The song helped to part the storm that had been raised by the *Tuatha Dé Danann* in an attempt to stop the Milesians from reaching the land.

The Book of Fercheirtne Filidh

Also known as 'The Dialogue of Two Sages', the story tells of a bardic battle between Fercheirtne and Nede for the position of chief bard or poet of Ireland. Both combatants display their poetic skill in a series of questions and answers that reveal encoded wisdom.

The Book of Cennfaeladh

Cenn Fáelad mac Ailella is an Irish scholar who fights in the Battle of Moira in 637 between the forces of the High King of Ireland vs. Ulaid. Ulaid was supported by Dál Riata as well as Scots, Saxons and Welshmen.

Cenn suffers a life threatening head wound in the battle and is then taken to the abbey of Tomregan to be healed, where he finds that his memory has improved remarkably.

4.4 *Tochmarc Étaíne* (The Wooing of Étaín / Éadaoin)

The *Tochmarc Étaíne* is part of the Irish Mythological Cycle which also features characters from the Ulster Cycle and the Cycles of the Kings. It is preserved in two manuscripts:

- *Lebor na hUidre* (Royal Irish Academy, MS 23 E 25, c1106) (partial)
- The 'Yellow Book of Lecan' (Trinity College Dublin, H. 2. 16., c1391-1401) (complete)

The story concerns Étaín, a beautiful mortal woman in the over-kingdom of *Ulaid* in north eastern Ireland and Aengus and Midir, who are members of the *Tuatha Dé Danann*.

In the story a druid named Dalan takes three wands of a yew tree and writes ogham letters on them, he then uses them for divination, but it is not mentioned how the sticks are handled or how their symbols are interpreted.

> *"Then, at the last, king Eochaid sent for his Druid, and he set to him the task to seek for Etain; now the name of the Druid was Dalan.*
>
> *And Dalan came before him upon that day; and he went westwards, until he came to the mountain that was after that known as Slieve Dalan; and he remained there upon that night.*
>
> *And the Druid deemed it a grievous thing that Etain should be hidden from him for the space of one year, and thereupon he made three wands of yew; and upon the wands he wrote an ogham; and by the keys of wisdom that he had, and by the ogham, it was revealed to him that Etain was in the fairy mound of Bri Leith, and that Mider had borne her thither".*

It is open to interpretation how the sticks were used for divination, but one theory is that the sticks were cast on to a cloth marked out with a pattern such as the *Fege Find* (Fionn's Window), and then the reading was interpreted by where the sticks land in relation to the pattern and each other.

Such readings and castings in modern paganism often involve interpreting the symbols with the folklore meanings of the trees that each letter represents, or by reference to one or more of the three Bríatharogaim.

5 The Celtic Calendar

Part of humankind's relationship with the earth and the cosmos is characterised by the marking of the celestial events, and their affect on nature, such as the changing of the seasons.

Evidence of early human beings recording lunar cycles by means of carvings on bones goes back 25,000 years, and between 4000 BCE and 2500 BCE the Neolithic agricultural revolution brought about a greater understanding of the changing of the seasons.

This is also true of the Celtic peoples, who marked these seasonal changes throughout the year with festivals and events such as *Samhain*, *Imbolc*, *Beltane*, and *Lugnasadh*, and the Spring Equinox, Summer Solstice, Autumn Equinox, and Winter Solstice.

5.1 The Coligny Calendar

The oldest known Celtic calendar is the Coligny calendar, so called because it was discovered in Coligny in eastern France in 1897.

It is a lunisolar calendar that was designed to reconcile the cycles of the moon and the sun, so that effectively the middle of each month would coincide with a full moon.

The Coligny Calendar, Gallo-Roman Museum of Lyon-Fourvière
Source: Wikipedia Creative Commons

The language of the text is Gaulish, one of the 'Continental Celtic' languages of continental Europe, but the text is inscribed in the Latin alphabet, including Roman numerals.

The calendar in the form of a bronze tablet was originally found broken into 73 pieces. The Roman Emperor Julius Ceaser had prohibited the use of any calendar within the empire other than his own Julian calendar, which would later be replaced by the Gregorian calendar which is still in use today in many parts of the world.

The Coligny calendar begins the year at *Samonios* (October / November), and there are twelve months, each with 29 or 30 days. There is an extra intercalary month inserted every 2 and a half years, either at the beginning of the year called '*Quimonios*', or in the middle of the year between '*Cutios*' and '*Giamonios*', with the name '*Sonnocingos*' meaning 'the sun's march'.

The term 'intercalary' is from the Latin *inter-* (between) + *calare* (to proclaim), i.e. to proclaim something as inserted in the calendar.

This is comparable to the leap year in the Gregorian calendar where an 'intercalary' extra day is added at the end of February every fourth year.

Begins	Ends	Days	Month	Meaning
Intercalary (Year 1)		30	*Quimonios*	Unknown
October	November	30	*Samonios*	Seeds falling
November	December	29	*Dumannios*	The darkest depths
December	January	30	*Riuros*	The cold time
January	February	29	*Anagantios*	Stay at home times
February	March	30	*Ogronios*	The time of ice
March	April	30	*Cutios*	The time of winds
Intercalary (Year 3)		30	*Sonnocingos*	The sun's march
April	May	29	*Giamonios*	Shoots and snow
May	June	30	*Simivisionios*	The time of brightness
June	July	29 or 30	*Equos*	Horse time
July	August	29	*Elembiuos*	Claim time
August	September	30	*Edrinios*	Arbritation time
September	October	20	*Cantios*	Song time

5.2 The 'Wheel of Year'

The Wheel of Year represents the yearly cycle of 'midpoints' (the fire festivals of *Samhain*, *Imbolc*, *Beltane*, and *Lugnasadh*) which are called 'cross quarter days', and also solar events (Spring Equinox, Summer Solstice, Autumn Equinox, and Winter Solstice) which are called 'quarter days'.

The names of these festivals vary between different pagan traditions, and the day or date of the events varies slightly, give or take one or two days, due to differences in lunar phase, and geographic location, particularly in relation to the hemisphere.

Some pagan traditions in the southern hemisphere shift the wheel by six months to align with local seasonal changes. The passage of time is referred to as 'the turning of the wheel'.

Fire Festivals

Samhain

Samhain or 'Samhna' meaning 'summer end' refers to the month of November, the arrival of which is celebrated on the 31st October, since the Celtic day began and ended at sunset rather than sunrise. This coincides with the eve of 'All Saints' Day', known as 'All Hallows Eve' or 'Hallowe'en'. This time of year is thought to be when the veil between the world of the living and the Otherworld is at its thinnest, and so the dead may return to warm themselves by the fires of the living. Also at this time members of the poet class believed that they could enter the Otherworld through special forts or 'sidhe' that acted as a gateway between the two worlds, such as the Hill of Tara near Skryne in County Meath, Ireland.

Imbolc

Imbolc or 'Oimelc' meaning 'Ewes milking' coincides with lambing time, traditionally around the 31st January. Women meet to celebrate the return of the maiden aspect of the goddess, symbolised by Brigid, a member of the *Tuatha Dé Danann* who is associated with wisdom, poetry, healing, protection, smithery, and domesticated animals. She is also associated with a perpetual sacred flame, similar to the Roman Vesta, and the Greek Hestia. Brigid was later adopted into Christianity through St Brigid of Kildare, a patron saint of Ireland.

Beltane

Beltane or 'Bealtane' meaning 'Bright fire' or 'Fires of Bel' refers to the month of May, celebrated on the 1st day of May, or 'May Day', as a time of abundance, feasts, and fertility. Cattle are let out and driven between two fires as a kind of cleansing ritual. Beltane is believed to derive from 'Bel-tinne', meaning 'the fires of Bel' referring to the ancient Celtic healing god 'Belenus', known in Gaulish as 'Belenos' or 'Belinos', and also as 'the Shining One'.

Lúgnasadh

Lúgnasadh or 'Lúnasa' meaning 'Lug's festival' refers to the month of August, and is also known as 'Brón Trogain'. Lúgnasad is related to the Celtic god Lugh, a member of the *Tuatha Dé Danann* who is associated with skill and mastery of the arts, truth and law, and rightful rule. The Romans are said to have identified Lugh with their own god Mercury, or Hermes in the Greek tradition.

Solar Festivals

Less is known about the Celtic pagan celebration of solar festivals. It is believed that the solstices were celebrated, particularly since motifs of sun disks and solar chariot wheels are found in Celtic art. However there appears to be a lack of surviving Celtic terms for these solar festivals.

The Anglo-Saxon settlement of Britain from c410 CE onwards resulted in a decline of Brythonic Celtic languages, and it is possible that during this decline, the Celtic terms for the solar festivals were lost and replaced by the equivalent Anglo-Saxon Germanic terms that remained. This theory could not however be stretched to account for a lack of Goidelic terms. It could also be that the Druids, the elite class of religious leaders of the Celtic peoples, focused on lunar events rather than solar events. However this is inconclusive due to the lack of written records.

'Ostara' is derived from the West Germanic goddess '*Ēostre*' related to 'Easter', and 'Mabon' for harvest time is a reference to the figure in Welsh mythology '*Mabon ap Modron*', known as '*Maponos*' (Great son) by the Gauls, and '*Modron*' meaning 'Great Mother', in this case perhaps meaning Great Mother Earth, to whom thanks is given for a good harvest.

Name	Anglo-Saxon	Modern English
Yule	*Gēol, Mōdraniht*	Yule, Mothers' Night
Midwinter	*Middanwinter*	Midwinter
Ostara	*Eastre*	Easter
Spring Equinox	*Efnight*	Even night
Litha	*Līþa*	Gentle, calm, navigable
Midsummer	*Middansumor*	Midsummer
Mabon	*Hæfest, Hærfest*	Harvest
Autumn Equinox	*Efnight*	Even night

- Samhain — New Year — 1st Nov
- Yule — Winter Solstice — 20th-23rd Dec
- Imbolc — Spring Begins — 1st Feb
- Ostara — Spring Equinox — 19th-22nd Mar
- Beltane — Summer Begins — 1st May
- Litha — Summer Solstice — 19th-23rd June
- Lughnasadh — Harvest Begins — 1st Aug
- Mabon — Autumn Equinox — 21st-24th Sep

6 The Celtic Revival and the Pagan Revival

At the end of the 18th century the Romantic Movement swept across Europe and inspired a great revival of interest in history, folklore, mythology, literature, and local traditions. These were rediscovered and celebrated as part of the complex and unique makeup of national identity. Scholars located, edited, and translated surviving manuscripts, artefacts, monuments, and other information. Research into Gaelic and Brittonic cultures in Great Britain helped to encourage a growing sense of Celtic identity.

This work provided the knowledge base and source material for the rediscovery, recreation, reconstruction, and revival of many diverse spiritual and religious movements. Some describe paganism as a movement divided into different religions, whereas some describe it as a single religion with different denominations. The academic field of Pagan studies is devoted to the study of this movement, and how it is influenced by or derived from belief systems of pre-modern Europe.

6.1 R. A. S. Macalister

Robert Alexander Stewart Macalister (8th July 1870 - 26th April 1950) was an Irish archaeologist. From 1909 to his retirement in 1943 he held the position of professor of Celtic archaeology at University College Dublin, translated texts of Irish mythology, and also published a catalogue of all known ogham inscriptions in Great Britain and Ireland (*Corpus Inscriptionum Insularum Celticarum*, 1945). Knowledge and interest in the ogham alphabet is greatly informed and influenced by his work.

R. A. S. Macalister, before 1950
Source: Wikipedia Creative Commons

Macalister also proposed that since the Ogham letters were collectively referred to as the '*Beith-Luis-Nin*', the correct order of the letters must have originally been '*Beith*', '*Luis*', '*Nin*', '*Fern*', '*Sail*' (BLNFS), rather than the '*Beith*', '*Luis*', '*Fern*', '*Sail*', '*Nin*' (BLFSN) that appears in manuscript sources. This has since been rejected by scholars.

6.2 Robert Graves

Robert von Ranke Graves (24th July 1895 - 7th December 1985) was a British poet, novelist, critic, classicist, and Celticist. In his work 'The White Goddess' he elaborated on the work of Macalister, while also drawing on the influence of the 17th century Irish historian Roderic O'Flaherty (*Ruaidhrí Ó Flaithbheartaigh*) to create his own poetic take on the history and traditions of the Celtic people, and the Ogham alphabet.

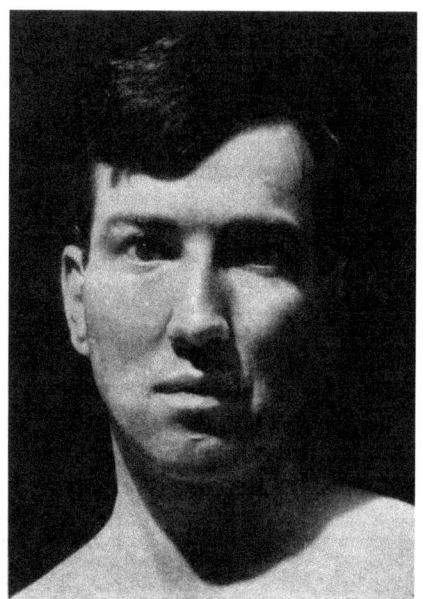

Robert Graves, 1929
Source: Wikipedia Creative Commons

Graves argues that the Ogham alphabet encodes a set of beliefs originating in the Middle East in Palaeolithic times, including ceremonies worshipping a moon goddess, which reached Ireland via the druids of Gaul, being passed on to the poets of early Ireland and Wales, including folklore for each letter that is represented by a tree, ultimately forming an ancient "*seasonal calendar of tree magic*".

> *"When recently I wrote on this subject to Dr MacAlister, as the best living authority on Oghams, he replied that I must not take O'Flaherty's alphabets seriously: 'They all seem to me to be late artificialities, or rather pedantries of little more importance than the affectations of Sir Pierce Shafton and his kind'. I pass on this caution in all fairness, for my argument depends on O' Flaherty's alphabet... I feel justified in supposing that O'Flaherty was recording a genuine tradition at least as old as the thirteenth century AD".[2]*

---

[2] Graves, R 'The White Goddess', Faber & Faber, London, 1948 (1961)

This drew criticism from scholars for his dismissal of the world's leading authority on the subject, his use of language in oral and written historical sources, and for relying on superseded archaeology to support his theories, namely:

- The correct order of the first five letters is *'Beith'*, *'Luis'*, *'Nin'*, *'Fern'*, *'Sail'*, as per Macalister's theory.
- All of the ogham letters are named after trees.
- There are 13 consonants in the ogham alphabet
- The 13 consonants and their trees correspond with 13 lunar months
- The ogham and their tree names are part of a *"seasonal calendar of tree magic*[3]*"*
- The 'Celtic Tree' calendar is the basis for 'Celtic astrology'

British historian Peter Beresford Ellis in his article 'The Fabrication of 'Celtic' Astrology' gives a detailed criticism of Graves's approach, adding that native Celtic cosmology was related to the Vedic tradition by their shared Indo-European origins, and at the beginning of Christianity, the Celtic world along with much of Western Europe converted to the Greco-Romano forms of astrology:

> *"Our earliest surviving Irish zodiacal chart dates to the 8th Century AD. Our earliest surviving texts on astrology and astronomy in Irish and Hiberno-Latin date back to the 7th Century. Gaulish Celts, writing in Latin as a lingua franca, were writing about astrology far earlier. Repositories, such as Trinity College, Dublin, are replete with astrological charts, texts and materials, and this is just the tip of a large linguistic iceberg for many such texts also survive throughout repositories in Europe where the Irish from the 7th Century established monastic sites and churches and carried their vast literary endeavours with them".*[4]

This is by no means the first time that a gap has opened up between the academic world and the world of spiritual and religious movements. The former of the two is the science of studying, collecting, and categorising evidence, supporting what we know to be fundamentally and self evidently true about the world we live in, telling the story of who we are and where we have come from. The latter is the product of thousands of years of belief, mythology, symbols of our relationship with the forces of nature, notions of the divine, an ever shifting and evolving syncretic cross-pollination of stories, told and re-told with different names, poems, songs, rituals, and the invention of deities that we create, shape, and choose to believe in.

People chose to believe in and adopt Graves's interpretations, presentations, and inventions on the subject, perhaps because the result of his work poetically packaged together a magical alphabet, magical tree folklore, a uniquely 'Celtic' calendar and zodiac, all tied together with the attractive symbolism of spirituality and nature.

---

[3] Graves, R 'The White Goddess', Faber & Faber, London, 1948 (1961)
[4] Ellis, Peter Beresford 'The Fabrication of 'Celtic' Astrology', The Astrological Journal (vol 39. n. 4, 1997)

Ogham 6. The Celtic and Pagan Revivals

6.3 Ogham Tree Meanings

No.		Letter	Name	Meanings
1		B	*BEITHE* *BEITH*	Birch tree *Betula pendula*
2		L	*LUIS* *LUIS*	Rowan tree *Sorbus aucuparia*
5		N	*NIN* *NION*	Ash tree *Fraxinus excelsior*
3		F	*FERN* *FEARN*	Alder tree *Alnus glutinosa*
4		S	*SAIL* *SAIL*	Willow tree *Salix alba*
6		H	*hÚATH* *UATH*	Whitethorn or Hawthorn plant *Crataegus punctata*
7		D	*DAIR* *DAIR*	Oak tree *Quercus robur*
8		T	*TINNE* *TINNE*	Holly tree *Ilex aquifolium*
9		C	*COLL* *COLL*	Hazel tree *Corylus avellana*
10		Q	*CERT* *CEIRT*	Apple tree *Malus sylvestris*
11		M	*MUIN* *MUIN*	Vine plant *Rubus villosus*
12		G	*GORT* *GORT*	Ivy plant *Hedera helix*
13		NG	*nGÉTAL* *NGÉADAL*	Broom, fern plant or reed *Phragmites australis*
14		Z	*STRAIPH* *STRAIF*	Blackthorn plant *Prunus spinosa*

No.		Letter	Name	Meanings
15		R	RUIS RUIS	Elder plant *Sambucus nigra*
16		A	AILM AILM	Pine tree *Ulmus procera*
17		O	ONN ONN	Ash tree, furze plant, or gorse *Ulex europaeus*
18		U	ÚR ÚR	Heather plant or blackthorn plant *Calluna vulgaris*
19		E	EDAD EADHADH	Aspen tree *Populus tremula*
20		I	IDAD IODHADH	Yew tree *Taxus baccata*
21		EA	EBHADH EABHADH	Aspen tree *Populus tremula*
22		OI	ÓR ÓR	Spindle tree or ivy *Eunonymus, Ulex europaeus*
23		UI	UILLEAND UILLEANN	Honeysuckle plant *Caprifoliaceae*
24		P IO	IPHIN PÍN IFÍN	Gooseberry or thorn plant *Ribes uva-crispa*
25		X Ch AE	EAMHANCHOLL EAMHANCHOLL	Hazel tree *Corylus avellana*
26		P	PEITH	Guelder rose plant *Viburnum opulus*

6.4   The Celtic Tree Calendar

The 'Celtic Tree' calendar devised by Robert Graves begins the year on the 24th December instead of the 31st October / 1st November. Presumably this is to align the beginning of the year with pagan celebrations of the birth of the sun god and the return from the darkness of winter to the light of spring. There are 13 months linked to sacred trees, each with its own corresponding ogham letter, except for the 23rd December, which is the one day that is not ruled by any tree.

With its symbolic alignment of months, seasons, sacred trees, branches, and ogham letters, it has the appeal of being tied to the natural world, which in modern times goes beyond concerns about whether or not it is actually how pre-modern Celtic people measured the sun, the moon, and the year. Rather, it is a combining of elements from the past in the spirit of the original traditions.

No.	Symbol	Letter	Name	Month / Moon	Begins	Ends
1		B	BEITHE BEITH	Birch	24 Dec	20 Jan
2		L	LUIS LUIS	Rowan	21 Jan	17 Feb
3		N	NIN NION	Ash	18 Feb	17 Mar
4		F	FERN FEARN	Alder	18 Mar	14 Apr
5		S	SAIL SAIL	Willow	15 Apr	12 May
6		H	hUATH UATH	Hawthorn	13 May	09 Jun
7		D	DAIR DAIR	Oak	10 Jun	07 Jul
8		T	TINNE TINNE	Holly	08 Jul	04 Aug
9		C	COLL COLL	Hazel	05 Aug	01 Sep
10		M	MUIN MUIN	Vine	02 Sep	29 Sep
11		G	GORT GORT	Ivy	30 Sep	27 Oct
12		GG	nGÉTAL NGÉADAL	Reed	28 Oct	23 Nov
13		R	RUIS RUIS	Elder	24 Nov	22 Dec

7 Divination

Divination is an attempt to gain insight into the will and intentions of the divine and the many forces operating around us that influence and shape our lives. The person asking the question or questions is the 'Querent', and the person who is consulting the ogham is the 'Reader'. If you are doing a reading for yourself, then you are both the Querent and the Reader.

There are different types of ogham sets, with different designs, made from different materials, even ogham oracle cards. They can be bought in shops specialising in esoteric, the occult, magic, and spirituality, and on specialist websites. Whether you are making your own ogham set or buying one, there are some choices to be made.

7.1   Deciding how many letters

Some people choose to use only the original 20 letters, referred to as 'Orthodox' Ogham. A historical argument for this could be that it is more authentic, since the *'Forfeda'* were added later to what would become known as 'Scholastic' Ogham as a useful way of transcribing Latin terms or loan words.

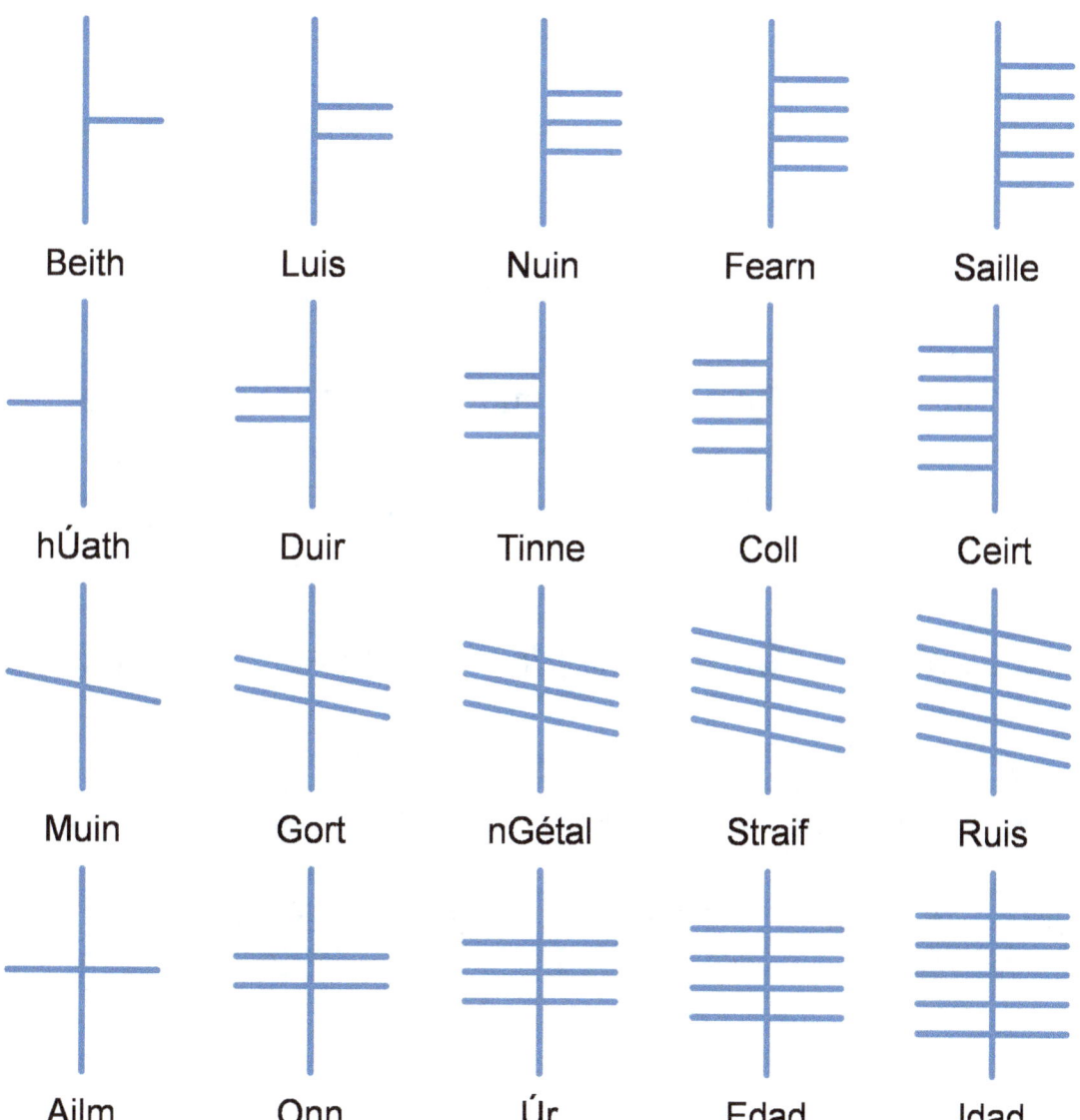

Ogham   *7. Divination*

Some people choose to include the *'Forfeda'* because the additional letters and their meanings add value to the reading. This takes the total number of letters up to 25 or 26.

The choice to include the *'Forfeda'* is similar to the choice available when reading runes. The original 'Elder Futhark' had 24 letters, the 'Younger Futhark' had 16, the 'Anglo-Saxon Futhorc' had up to 33, and the 'Icelandic Futhark' had 24 which included letters added as late as the 15th and 16th centuries. The Book of Ballymote even mentions the runes as a kind of ogham of the northmen.

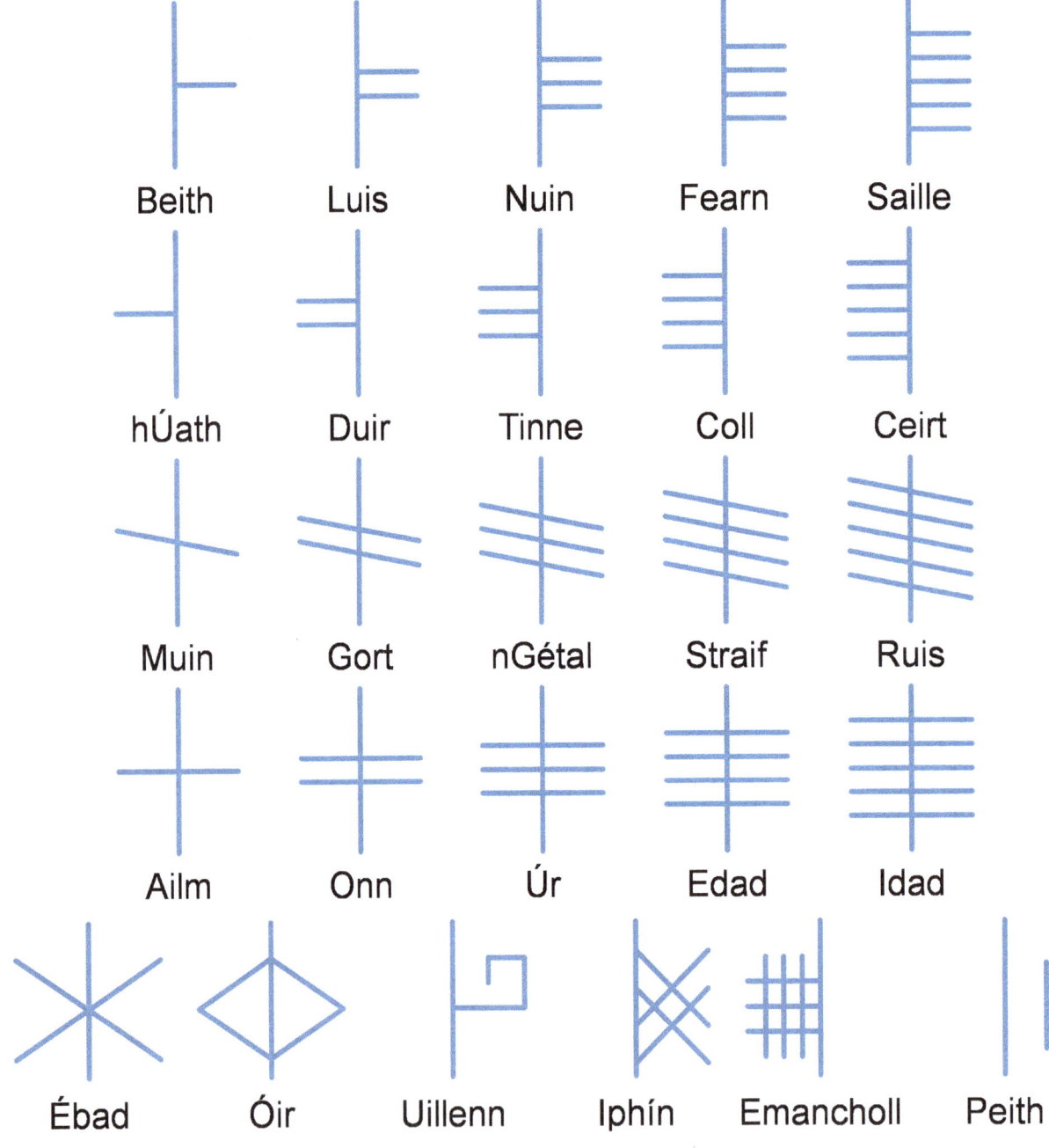

7.2 Distinguishing which way up the letters are

The first thing you may notice is that the 5 letters of the first *aicme* when rotated 180 degrees look exactly like the 5 letters of the second *aicme*.

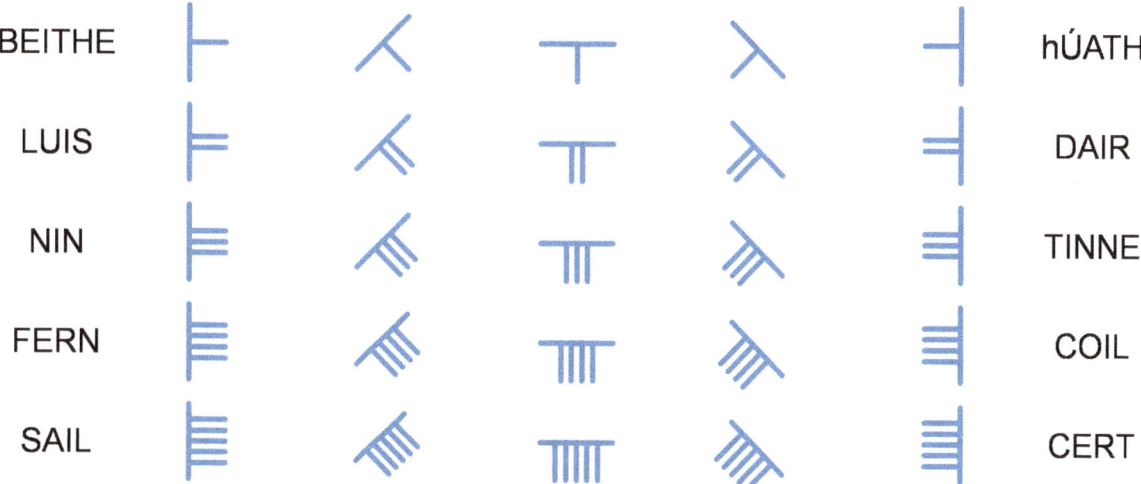

With this in mind, it becomes necessary to be able to distinguish the letters from each other and which way up they are.

7.3 Reversed letters

Some people choose to make a note of which letters appear upside down or 'reversed' in a reading, but some choose not to.

If you choose to make a note of reversed letters, the other thing you will notice is that the next 10 letters in the third and fourth *aicme* when rotated 180 degrees look exactly the same either way up.

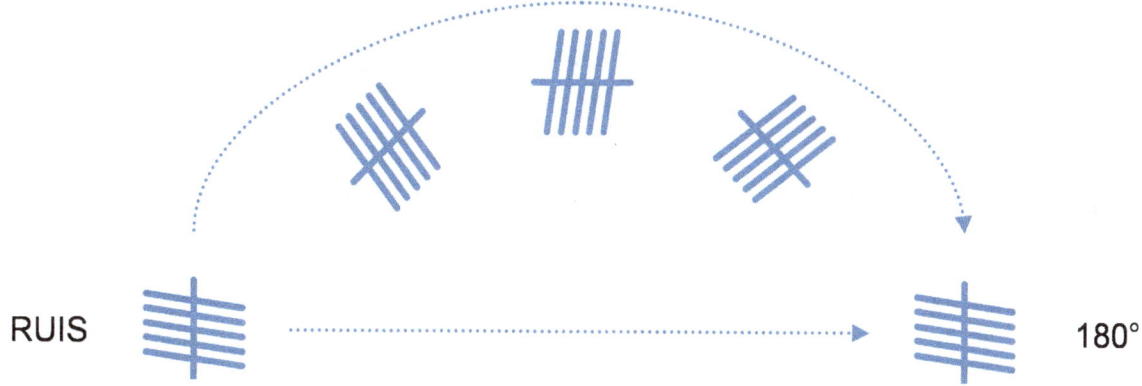

There are several ways the ogham can be designed to distinguish which way up each letter is.

Ogham 7. Divination

In this example, a small dot is marked above each letter to show where the top is.

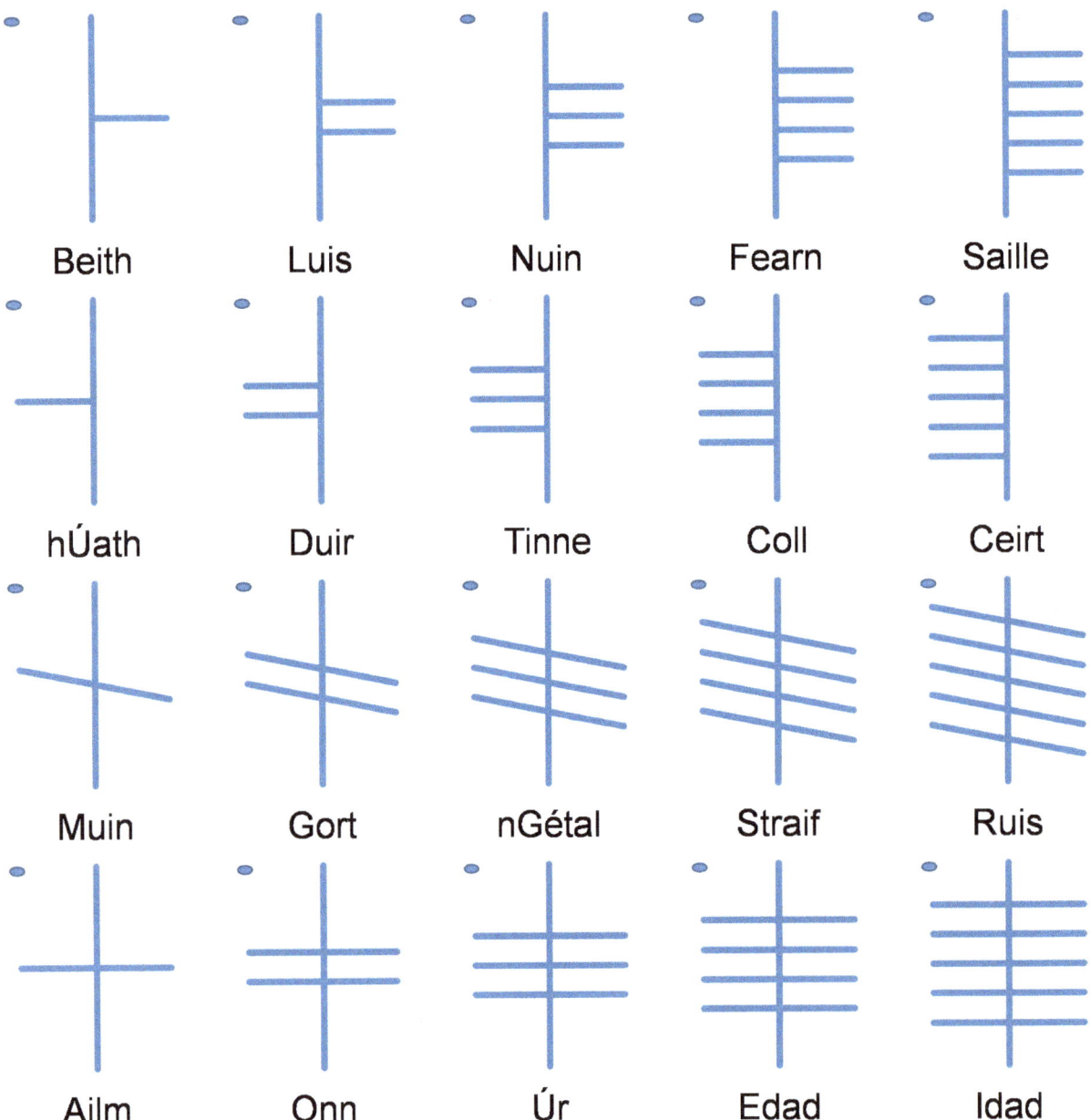

Ogham 7. *Divination*

In this example, a small line has been marked underneath each letter to show where the bottom is.

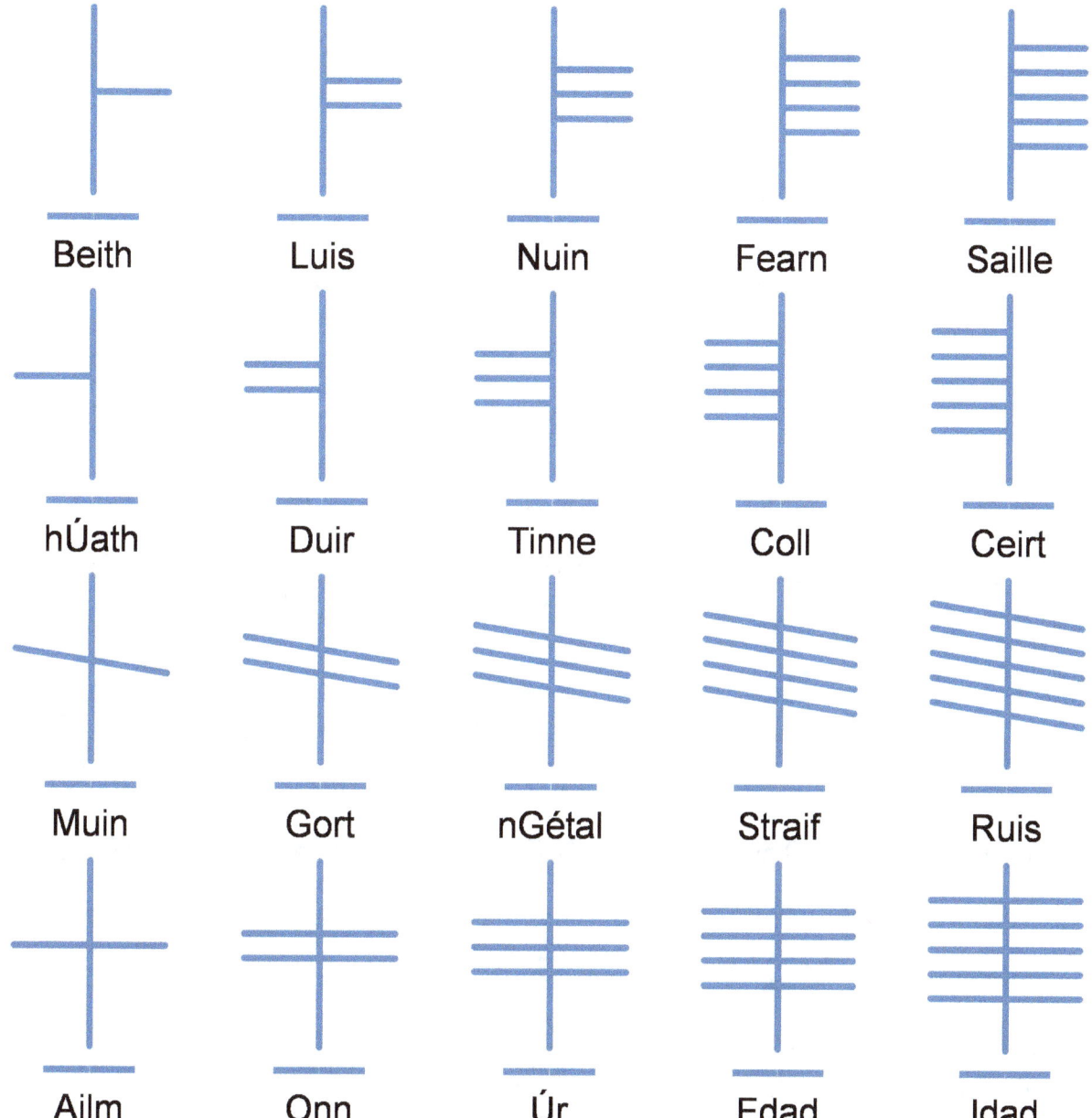

Ogham 7. Divination

In this example, an '*Eite*' or 'feather' has been added to the bottom of each letter to show where the bottom is.

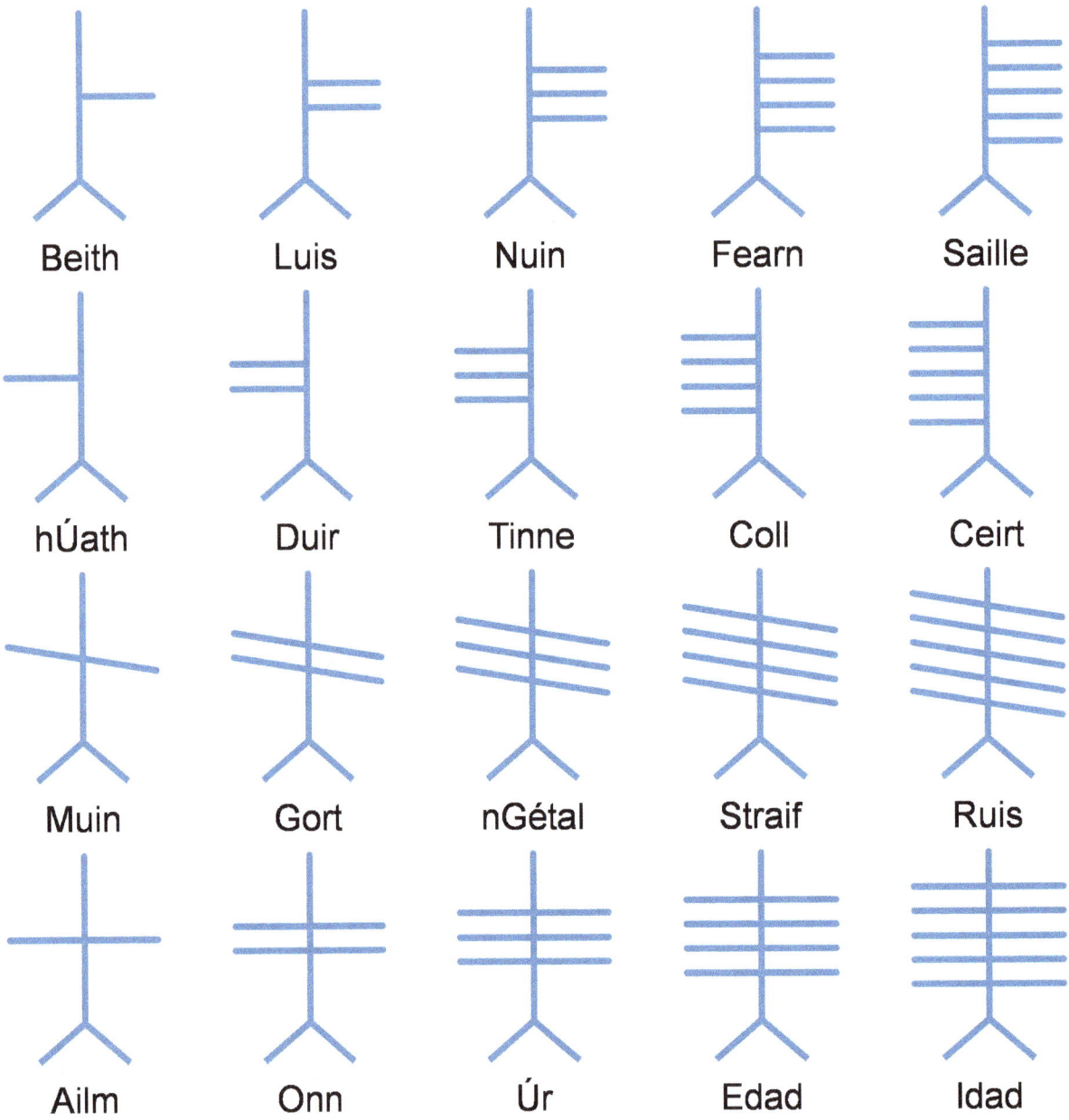

Ogham   *7. Divination*

If you are making your own set with sticks or twigs you may want to decide whether to shave or plane the surface of the stick at the top end so it is always clear which way up the letters are without using dots, lines, or feathers.

If the letter in question is rotated more than 90 degrees in either direction away from its perfect vertical position, it can be said to be reversed.

Upright

Reversed

Ogham   *7. Divination*

7.4 Selecting what material to use

Ogham inscriptions were originally carved in stone, so choosing or making a set in stone is a valid choice. Since ogham has also been closely associated with trees, wood is also a good choice.

It is possible to buy ogham sets with each twig being made of the associated wood relating to each symbol. This luxury adds symbolic meaning to the 'tree magic' aspect of ogham. However, this is not essential, as in the *Tochmarc Étaíne* mentioned earlier; the druid Dalal uses the yew tree for his three wands. Yew is a good choice, but wood from any fruit bearing tree is also suitable.

If you are using wooden discs instead of sticks, it is possible to buy the discs from craft shops and websites. For their use in arts and crafts the discs are sometimes supplied with small holes drilled through them. The small hole can be used in the same way as a marked dot to distinguish the top of each symbol and whether or not it is the right way up or reversed.

'Orthodox' Ogham burnt onto wooden discs

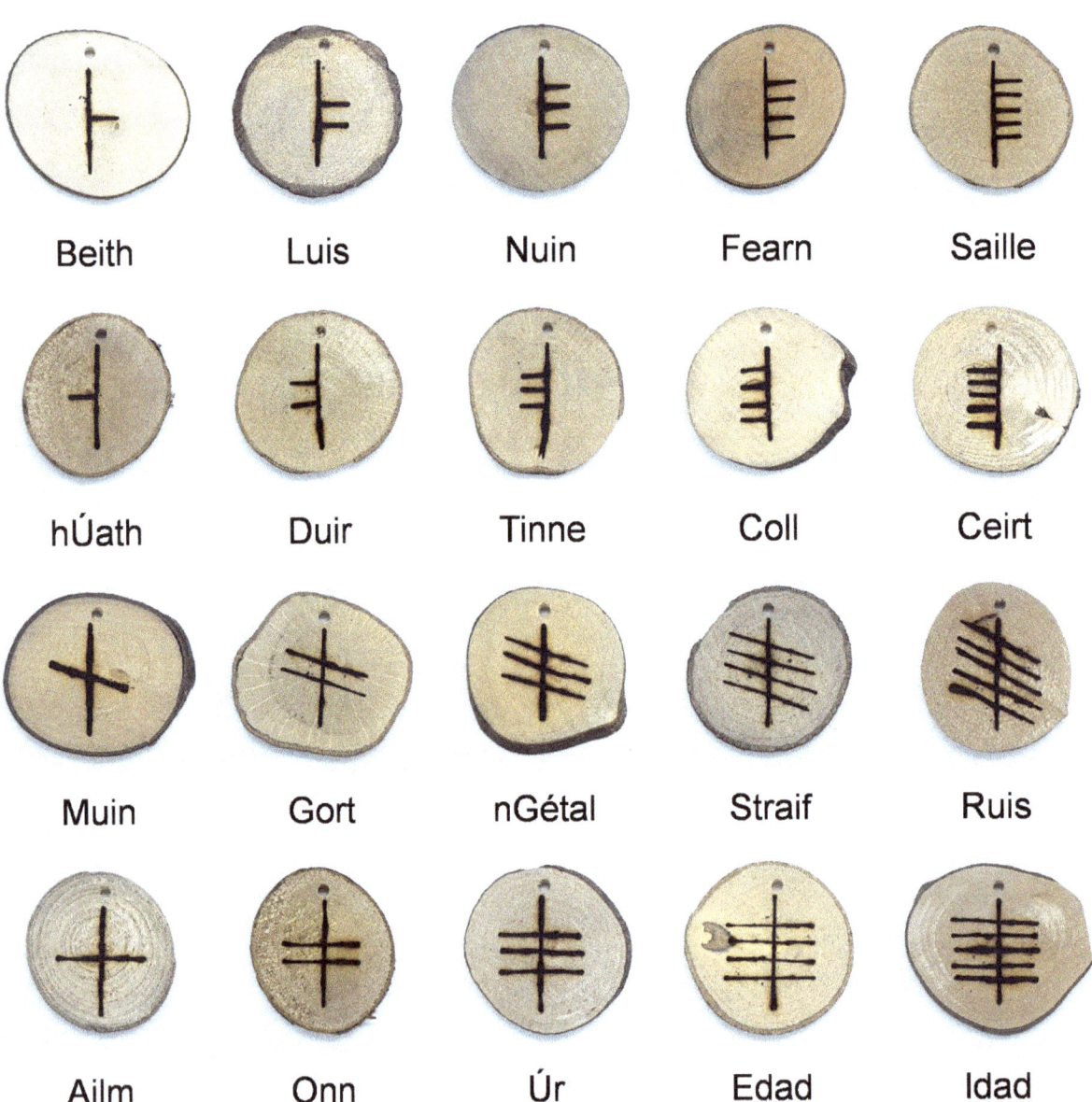

Ogham   7. Divination

'Scholastic' ogham burnt onto wooden discs

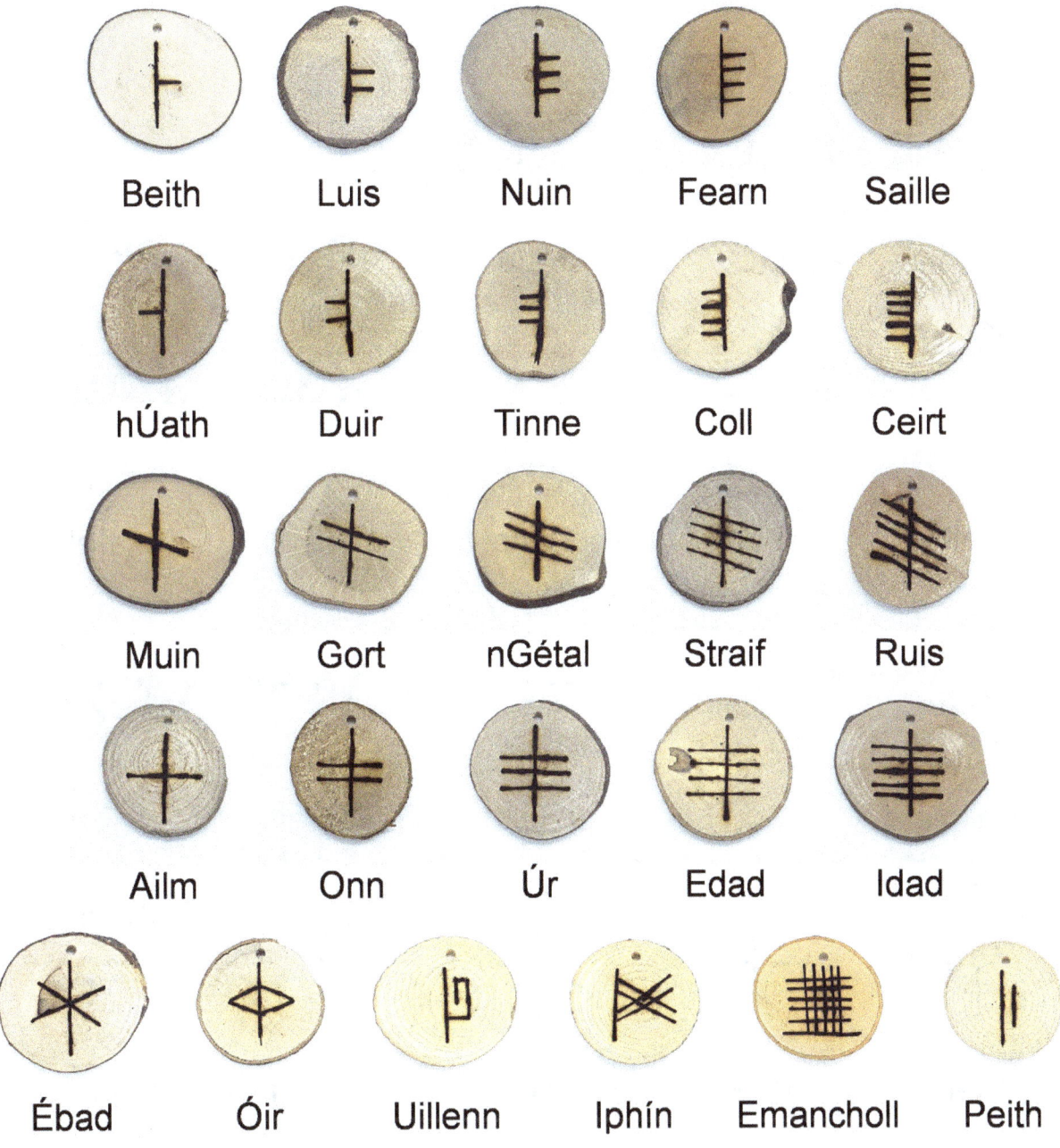

Ogham   *7. Divination*

'Orthodox' 'Sacred Branch' Ogham burnt onto wooden discs

Note: The Sacred Branch ogham appears in the Book of Ballymote as untitled (89). The name 'Sacred Branch' was added later, perhaps due to its resemblance to branches and trees, lending itself to Celtic tree mythology and divination.

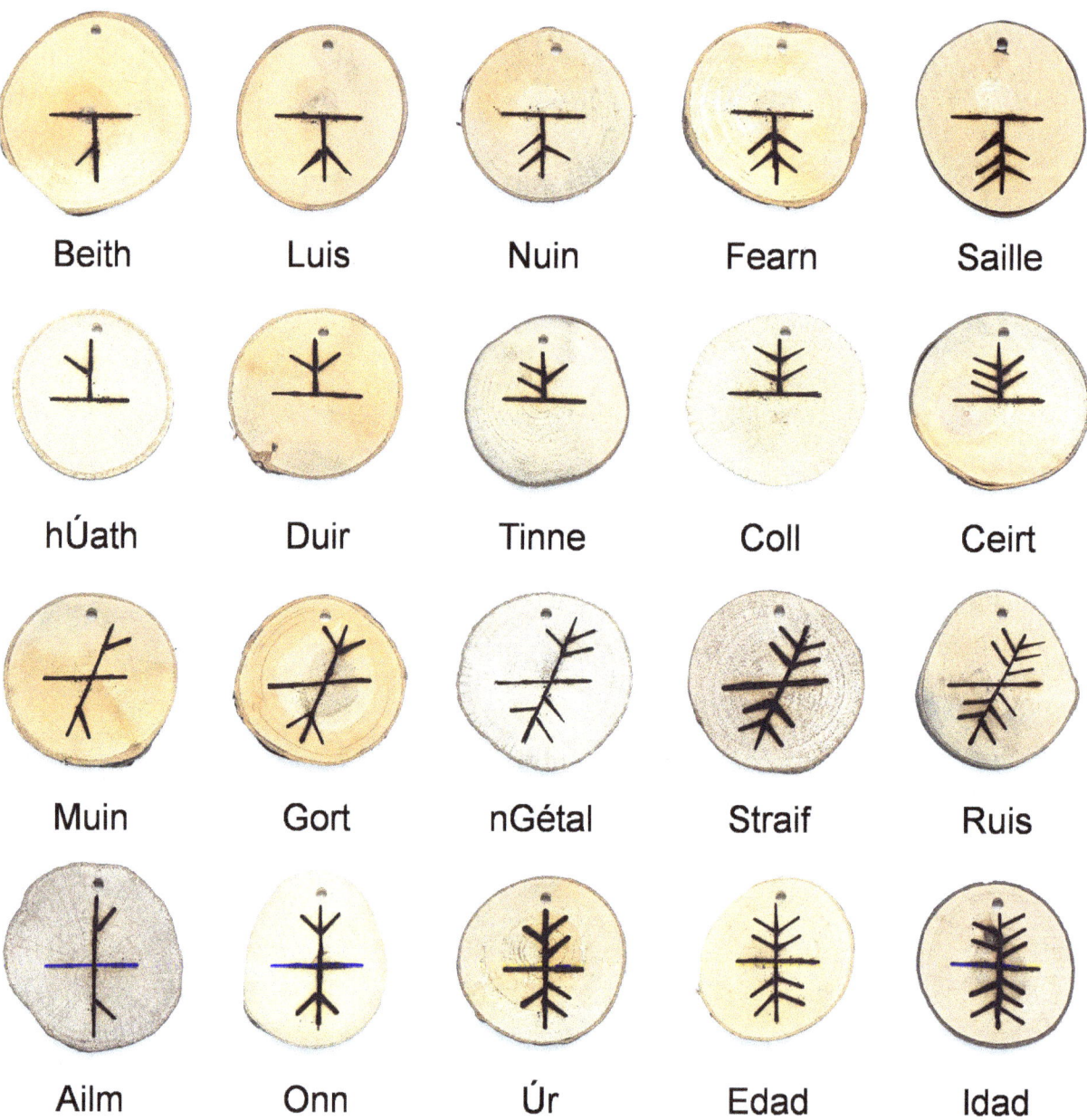

Ogham *7. Divination*

'Scholastic' Sacred Branch ogham burnt onto wooden discs

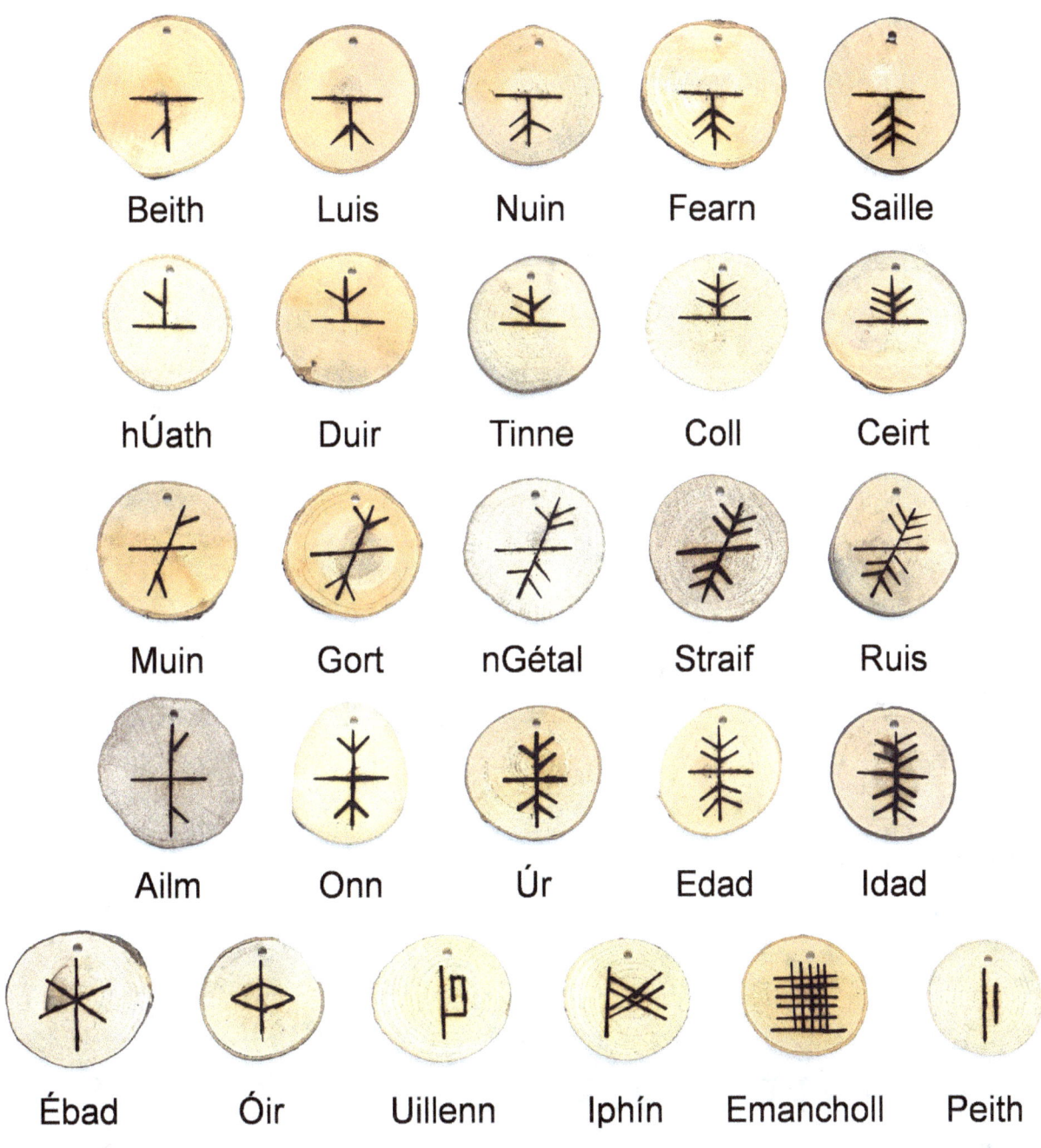

Ogham 7. Divination

7.5 Types of reading

Three ogham reading

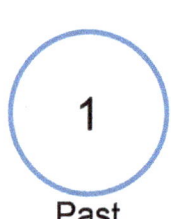 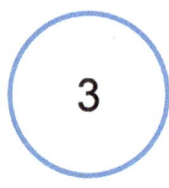

1	2	3
Past	Present	Future
Cause	Effect	Solution
Action	Challenge	Overview

Four ogham 'Hidden Truth' reading

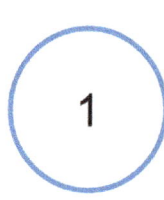 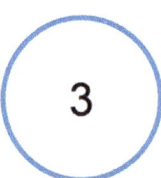 

1	2	3	4
What is the truth behind this situation?	How does this affect me?	Why has this been hidden from me?	How do I deal with this new information?

Five ogham V reading

 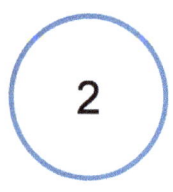 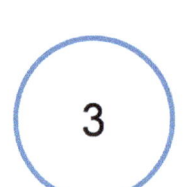 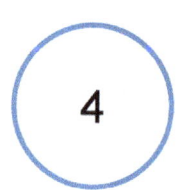 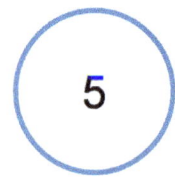

1	2	3	4	5
Past	Present	Future	Help	Problems
Overview	Challenge	New Situation	Action	Sacrifice

Ogham 7. *Divination*

Six ogham reading

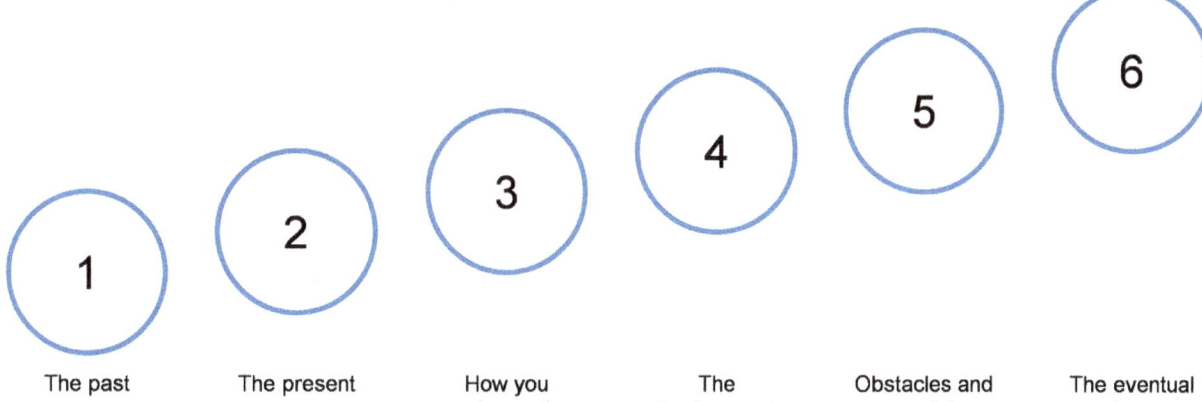

Seven ogham V reading

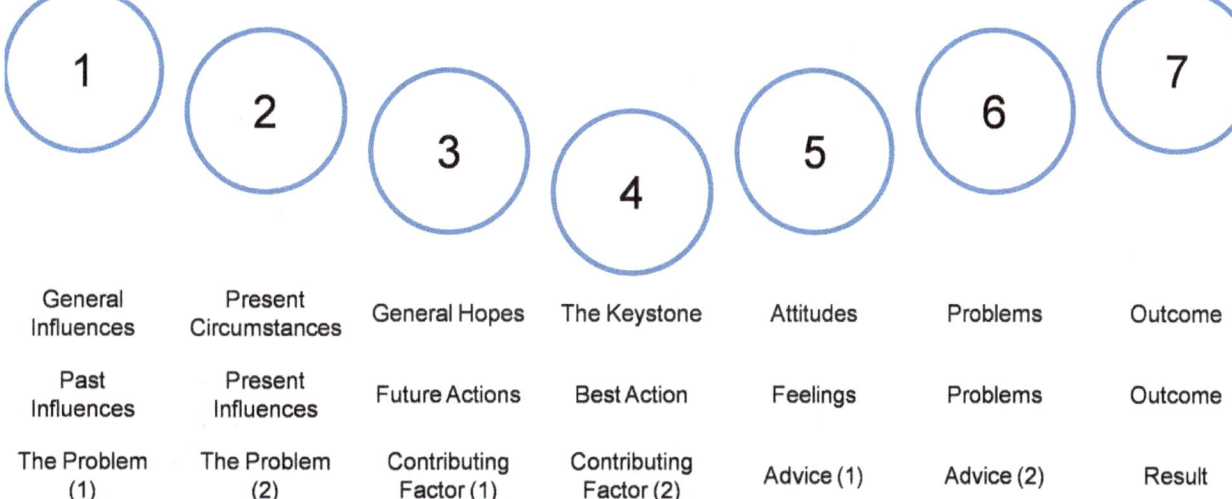

Nine ogham V reading

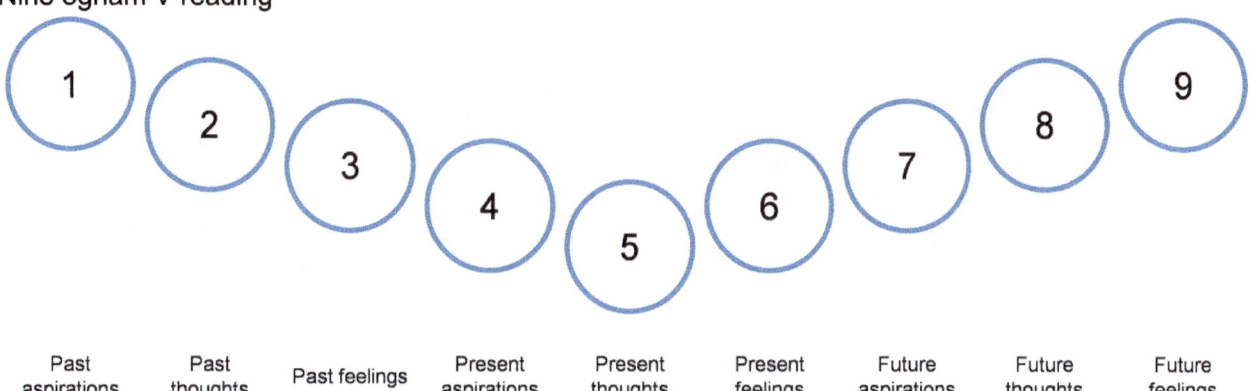

Ogham *7. Divination*

The 'Celtic Cross' spread

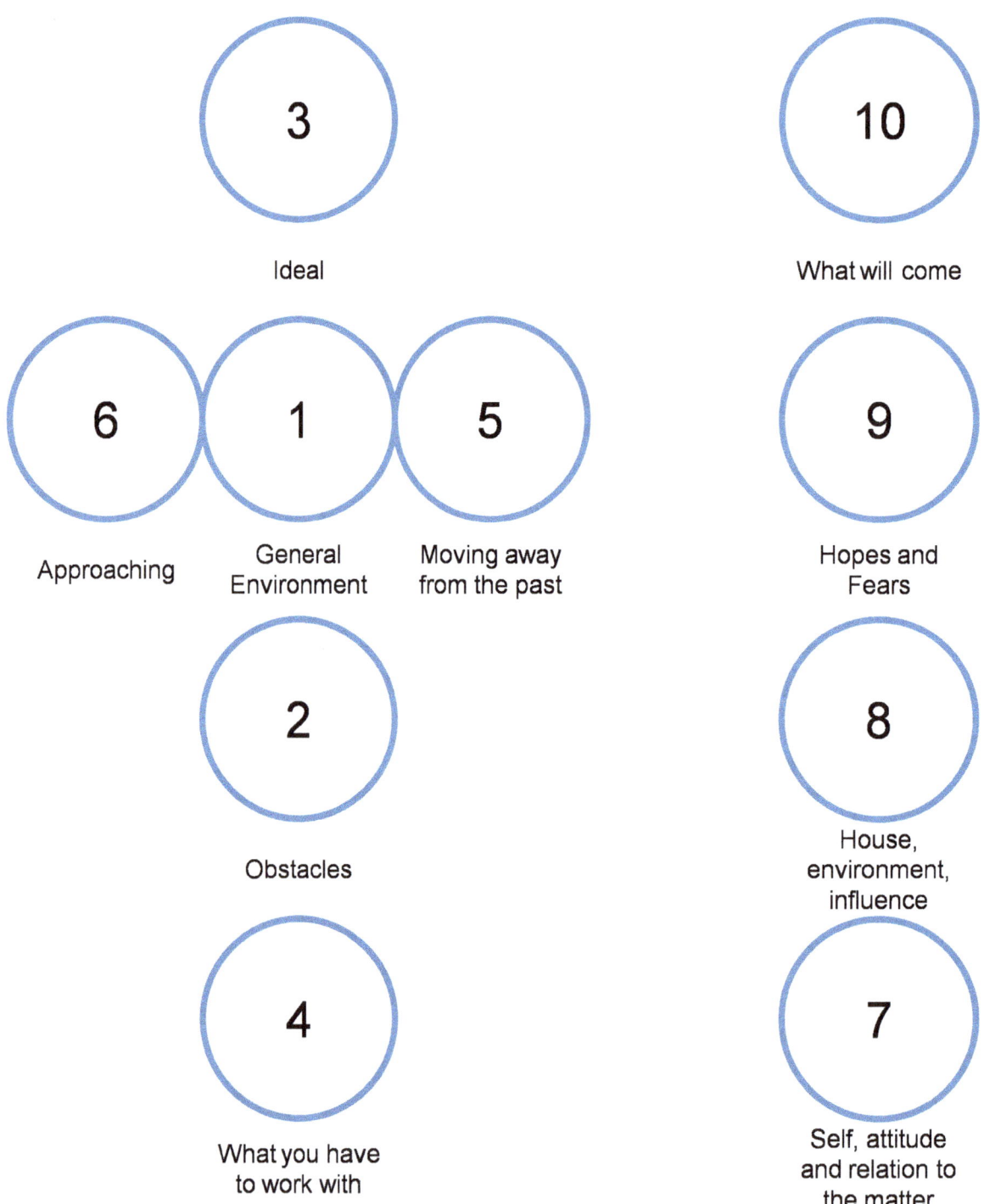

7.6 Casting

The object of casting is to gather a small amount of ogham at random from their ogham pouch while meditating on the question or issue, and then casting the ogham over the cloth letting them land where they may, and then interpreting the constellation of meaning that they create.

Once the ogham have landed, any of the ogham that are face down are turned the right way up. If you are taking note of the reversal of ogham, take care when turning the ogham the right way up, by turning it on its horizontal axis rather than its vertical one, or the ogham and its meaning will be reversed. This works best if your ogham are flat and regular in shape, otherwise this may not be possible.

A white cloth or material is preferable because it allows you to see the ogham and the shape of how they have landed more clearly. The cloth can be marked with inner and outer circles representing the distant and close matters, with the centre of the circle representing now. Compass points as indicated below can provide a cross-section of issues from positive to negative, and past, present, and future.

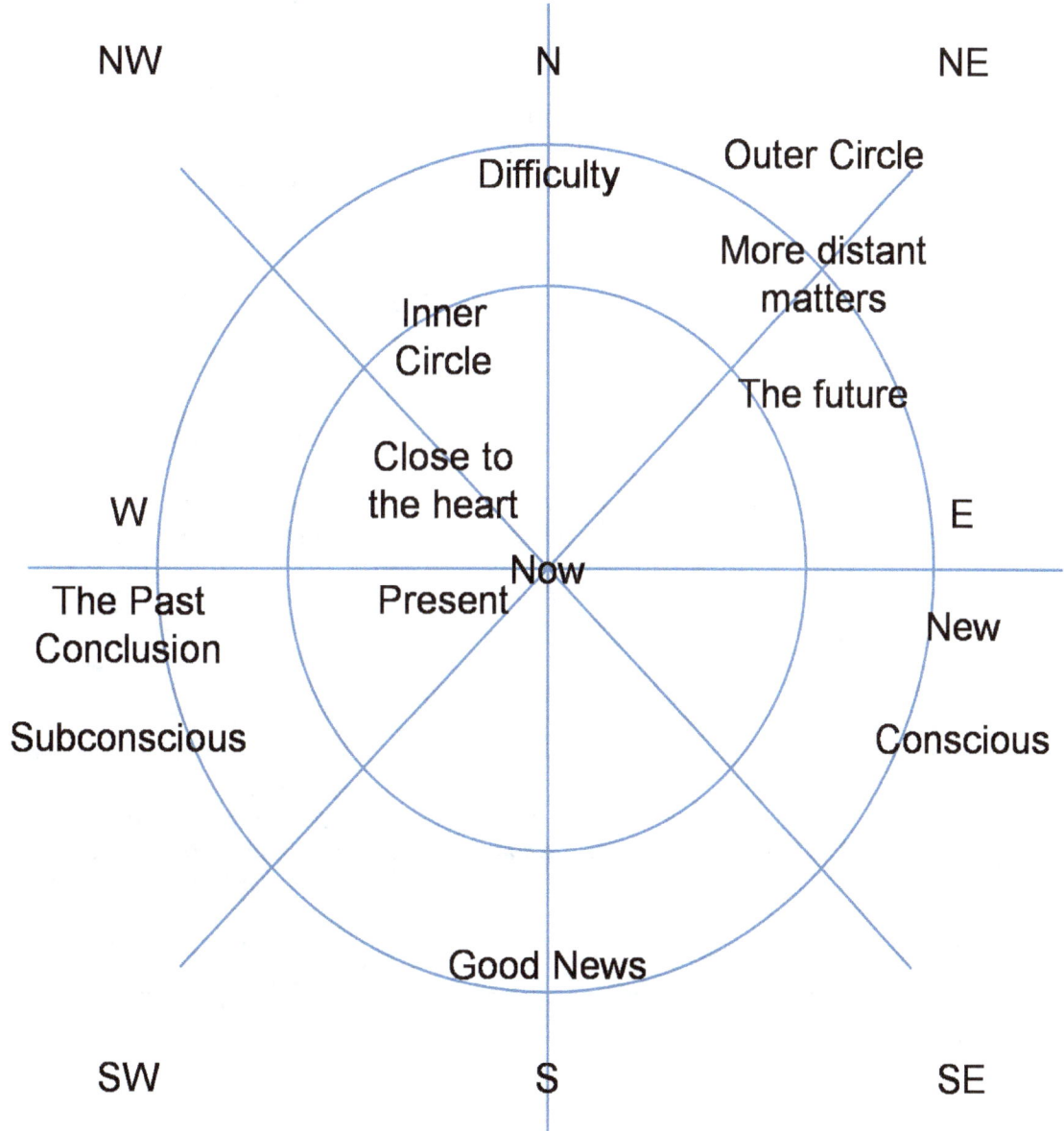

7.7 Meanings for Divination

No.		Letter	Name	Tree meaning	Divination meaning
1	┝	B	*BEITHE* *BEITH*	Birch tree *Betula pendula*	Changes, new beginnings, prepare for changes ahead. Reversed: Standing still, stuck in the past, let go of negativity to move forward.
2	┝	L	*LUIS* *LUIS*	Rowan tree *Sorbus aucuparia*	Defending against threats, growth, fresh ideas, creativity and inspiration. Reversed: Vulnerability, susceptibility to negativity, be cautious.
5	┝	N	*NIN* *NION*	Ash tree *Fraxinus excelsior*	Transitions, renewal, feminine strength, growth, peace, supportive friendships, fate. Reversed: A need to take control of your life, locate the root of problems.
3	┝	F	*FERN* *FEARN*	Alder tree *Alnus glutinosa*	Spiritual guidance, creativity, choices, emotional security, seek advice, gather knowledge. Reversed: Stubbornness, disregarding advice, hitting a creative wall.
4	┝	S	*SAIL* *SAIL*	Willow tree *Salix alba*	Balance, intuition, the cycle of the moon, astrological alignment, emotions, flowing water. Reversed: Feeling defeated, distracted, or lost.
6	┥	H	*hÚATH* *UATH*	Whitethorn or Hawthorn plant *Crataegus punctata*	Barriers, despair, protection, loneliness, strife, feeling suffocated. Reversed: Impasse, standstill.
7	┥	D	*DAIR* *DAIR*	Oak tree *Quercus robur*	Strength, security, resilience, endurance, wisdom, sacred spaces, leadership, and kindness. Reversed: Cowardliness, uncertain, frail, unkind or unfair leadership.
8	┥	T	*TINNE* *TINNE*	Holly tree *Ilex aquifolium*	Expertise, analysis, protection, transformation, skill, talent, overcoming action against you. Reversed: Attack, hardship, aggression.

No.		Letter	Name	Tree meaning	Divination meaning
9		C	COLL COLL	Hazel tree *Corylus avellana*	Enlightenment, knowledge, creative inspiration, daydreaming, rituals, proficiency, and practicality. Reversed: Ignorance, insensitivity, creative barriers.
10		Q	CERT CEIRT	Apple tree *Malus sylvestris*	Physical and mental wellness, rest, wholeness, spiritual harmony, and choices. Reversed: Despair, ailments, and overall unhappy energy.
11		M	MUIN MUIN	Vine plant *Rubus villosus*	Reaping what you have sown, goals coming to fruition, persuasion, celebration, relaxing, harvesting, and play. Reversed: Indulgence, lack of self discipline, dishonesty, tall tales.
12		G	GORT GORT	Ivy plant *Hedera helix*	Spirals, tenacious, wildness, development, abundance, gratitude, rest, and reawakening. Reversed: Difficulty, challenging forces outside, use your energy wisely.
13		NG	nGÉTAL NGÉADAL	Broom, fern plant or reed *Phragmites australis*	Health, vitality, strength, healing wounds, healers, and herbal remedies. Reversed: Sickness, illness, pain, suffering, lack of wellness, physically, mentally, or spiritually.
14		Z	STRAIPH STRAIF	Blackthorn plant *Prunus spinosa*	Unexpected changes, challenges, courage and fortitude. Reversed: Failure to adapt to change, move on, and be reborn.
15		R	RUIS RUIS	Elder plant *Sambucus nigra*	Shame, jealousy, obsession, remorse, vengeance, and retributive justice, letting go of vengeful thoughts. Reversed: Lack of self-reflection work, being in denial.
16		A	AILM AILM	Pine tree *Ulmus procera*	Joy, excitement, euphoria, creation, fertility, spiritual awakenings. Reversed: Paralysing fear, panic, or anxiety.

No.		Letter	Name	Tree meaning	Divination meaning
17		O	ONN ONN	Ash tree, furze plant, or gorse *Ulex europaeus*	Spiritual paths and guidance, movement, lust. Reversed: Complications, unhealthy behaviour, and danger.
18		U	ÚR ÚR	Heather plant or blackthorn plant *Calluna vulgaris*	Relationships, connections, good luck, death, graveyards, magic, reflection, connection with the earth. Reversed: Deception, deceit, disagreements, conflict.
19		E	EDAD EADHADH	Aspen tree *Populus tremula*	Bravery, defeating fear, perception, and divination. Reversed: Defeat, terror, addictive behaviour.
20		I	IDAD IODHADH	Yew tree *Taxus baccata*	Beginnings and endings, connecting with ancestors, meditation, contemplation. Reversed: Blocked from healing, regenerating, and moving on.
21		EA	EBHADH EABHADH	Aspen tree *Populus tremula*	Spiritual wisdom, strength, intelligence, transcending
22		OI	ÓR ÓR	Spindle tree or ivy *Eunonymus, Ulex europaeus*	Abundance, creativity, family, loved ones, and community.
23		UI	UILLEAND UILLEANN	Honeysuckle plant *Caprifoliaceae*	Resilience, change, chasing dreams, private thoughts, exposing secrets.
24		P IO	IPHIN PÍN IFÍN	Gooseberry or thorn plant *Ribes uva-crispa*	Everyday life, vision, divination, and releasing emotions of guilt or shame.
25		X Ch AE	EAMHANCHOLL EAMHANCHOLL	Hazel tree *Corylus avellana*	Meaning – disease or illness or need to purify or cleanse negative energy.
26		P	PEITH	Guelder rose plant *Viburnum opulus*	The metaphysical, symbology, seeing beyond, ancient knowledge, psychic protection, rebirth.

8 Magic

Magic works because we believe that it works. We believe in the process of signalling and communicating our intentions and desirable outcomes to the forces around us, releasing them into the universe, and having the confidence and belief to make it happen.

Whereas in divination we use the ogham to ascertain the will and intention of forces around us, in ogham magic we create our desired ogham reading, and will it into being. We program the reading that we would wish to have.

Placing

You can place the ogham around your shrine or in an equally special space.
You can place ogham where you would wish them to work, i.e. over a doorway for protection, etc.
You can wear ogham as talismans or pendants or in your clothing or carry them with you.

Activating

You can use candles to light up the ogham and to signal your desires and intentions.
You can use incense to help carry those intentions into the air.
You can use the power of the moon, a powerful symbolic embodiment of dreams and desires by placing your intentions on the night of a new moon, and then reviewing the outcome and success on the night of the following full moon.
You can whisper or chant the names of the ogham you are using during meditation or ritual.

Maintaining

You can maintain your ogham by:
- Placing them under the light of a full moon.
- Passing them one by one over incense smoke.
- Whispering or chanting the name of each ogham.

The following table describes the different ways in which ogham can be used for magical purposes.

8.1 Meanings for Magic

No.		Letter	Name	Tree meaning	Magical meaning
1		B	*BEITHE* *BEITH*	Birch tree *Betula pendula*	Fresh beginnings, overcoming challenging moments, cleansing energies, body, or space, love magic, renewal, fertility.
2		L	*LUIS* *LUIS*	Rowan tree *Sorbus aucuparia*	Protection, safety, calling on ancestors or departed loved ones for protection, sacred locations, protected by dragons and snakes.
5		N	*NIN* *NION*	Ash tree *Fraxinus excelsior*	Manifesting desires and intentions, inspiring imagination, creativity, new perspectives, spiritual and emotional healing.

No.		Letter	Name	Tree meaning	Magical meaning
3		F	FERN FEARN	Alder tree *Alnus glutinosa*	Calm when emotionally overwhelmed, connecting with the universe, ether, or otherworld, attracting prophetic dreams, and good advice.
4		S	SAIL SAIL	Willow tree *Salix alba*	The magic of the moon, cyclical intentions, fluidity, water, intuition, flexibility.
6		H	hÚATH UATH	Whitethorn or Hawthorn plant *Crataegus punctata*	Clearing negativity, encouraging intuition, insight, patience, wisdom, empathy, a protective barrier.
7		D	DAIR DAIR	Oak tree *Quercus robur*	Confidence, courage, good luck, protection during storms, healing, aiding memory, resilience, and strength.
8		T	TINNE TINNE	Holly tree *Ilex aquifolium*	Protection of the home, adapting to change, finding perspective, and creative inspiration.
9		C	COLL COLL	Hazel tree *Corylus avellana*	Meditation, creative inspiration, insight, knowledge, manifesting dreams and intentions.
10		Q	CERT CEIRT	Apple tree *Malus sylvestris*	Meditation, spiritual awakening, prosperity, healing, positive energy, shielding from negativity.
11		M	MUIN MUIN	Vine plant *Rubus villosus*	Seeking creative inspiration, inner growth, seeking truth, spiritual wisdom, and communication.
12		G	GORT GORT	Ivy plant *Hedera helix*	Strength, support, eliminating toxicity, harmony, creativity.
13		NG	nGÉTAL NGÉADAL	Broom, fern plant or reed *Phragmites australis*	Healing, meditation, cleansing a space of negativity, health or physical well-being.
14		Z	STRAIPH STRAIF	Blackthorn plant *Prunus spinosa*	Overcoming adversity, interpretation of omens, secrecy, connection with spirits and the Otherworld. Confronting challenges head on, support during change, finding the path ahead, guidance.
15		R	RUIS RUIS	Elder plant *Sambucus nigra*	Seeking wisdom, knowledge, self-transformation, and healing.
16		A	AILM AILM	Pine tree *Ulmus procera*	Seeking intuition, spiritual awareness, understanding, spiritual growth, and connection with the cosmos, attracting a positive mindset, connecting with ancestors, ease pains during pregnancy and childbirth.

No.		Letter	Name	Tree meaning	Magical meaning
17		O	ONN ONN	Ash tree, furze plant, or gorse *Ulex europaeus*	Safe journeys, physical movement, removing obstacles from your path.
18		U	ÚR ÚR	Heather plant or blackthorn plant *Calluna vulgaris*	Removing unwanted negativity, cleansing a space, good luck in battle.
19		E	EDAD EADHADH	Aspen tree *Populus tremula*	Communicating with the universe or the spirit world, releasing negative emotions, preparation for change, placing intentions, shielding, preventing danger.
20		I	IDAD IODHADH	Yew tree *Taxus baccata*	Help from ancestors, history, coming to terms with death, endings and new beginnings.
21		EA	EBHADH EABHADH	Aspen tree *Populus tremula*	Spiritual wisdom, strength and intelligence to rise above everyday problems, enlightenment, spiritual contentment, and harmony.
22		OI	ÓR ÓR	Spindle tree or ivy *Eunonymus, Ulex europaeus*	Abundance, creativity, honouring family, loved ones and community.
23		UI	UILLEAND UILLEANN	Honeysuckle plant *Caprifoliaceae*	Resilience, change, achieving your dreams, discovering secrets.
24		P IO	IPHIN PÍN IFÍN	Gooseberry or thorn plant *Ribes uva-crispa*	Enjoying day to day life, vision, divination, releasing negative emotions.
25		X Ch AE	EAMHANCHOLL EAMHANCHOLL	Hazel tree *Corylus avellana*	Purification, cleansing, removing negative energy.
26		P	PEITH	Guelder rose plant *Viburnum opulus*	Farsightedness, seeing beyond the obvious and every day, sight beyond sight, invocation, spells, ritual, celebration of life, psychic protection, offering peace, warding off incoming danger, birth, death and rebirth, protection during sleep.

9 Inscriptions

The following are selected from Macalister's '*Corpus Inscriptionum Insularum Celticarum*', where each inscription is given a 'CIIC' reference number.

9.1   Common Features

MAQI	┼·┉┅	'son'
MUCOI	┼┉┅┅	'tribe'
ANM	┅┉/	'name'
AVI	┉┅	'descendant'
CELI	┅┉┅	'follower' or 'devotee'
NETA	┉┅┉	'nephew'
KOI	✕┅	'here is'

9.2   Ireland

Ratass Church, Tralee, County Kerry
Source: Wikipedia Creative Commons

CIIC Ref.	Location	Text / Transliteration / Translation
1	Inchagoill Island, County Galway	LIE LUGNAEDON MACCI MENUEH "The stone of Lugnaedon son of Limenueh".
2	Bornacoola, County Leitrim	QENUVEN[DI] Qenuvendi, "white head", (Cenond, Cenondÿn, Cenindÿn)
3	Island, Costello, County Mayo	CUNALEGI AVI QUNACANOS "Cunalegi, descendant of Qunacanos"
4	Kilmannia, Costello, County Mayo	LUGADDON MA[QI] L[U]GUDEC DDISI MO[--]CQU SEL "Lugáed son of Luguid"

CIIC Ref.	Location	Text / Transliteration / Translation
5	Rusheens East, Kilmovee, Costello, County Mayo	ALATTOS MAQI BR["Alattos son of Br..."
6	Tullaghaun, Costello, County Mayo	QASIGN[I]MAQ[I] "Qasignias son of ..."
7	Corrower, Gallen, County Mayo	MAQ CERAN[I] AVI ATHECETAIMIN "Son of Ciarán, descendant of the Uí Riaghan"
8	Dooghmakeon, Murrisk, County Mayo	MA[QUI MUCOI] CORBAGNI GLASICONAS "Son of the tribe Corbagnus Glasiconas"
9	Aghaleague, Tirawley, County Mayo	MAQACTOMAQGAR "Son of Acto, son of Gar"

CIIC Ref.	Location	Text / Transliteration / Translation
10	Breastagh, Tirawley, County Mayo	L[E]GG[--]SD[--] LEGwESCAD MAQ CORRBRI MAQ AMMLLOGwITT "Legwescad, son of Corrbrias, son of Ammllogwitt"
38	Ballyboodan, Knocktopher, County Kilkenny	CORBI KOI MAQI LABRID "Here is Corb, son of Labraid"
47	Castletimon, Brittas Bay, County Wicklow	NETACARI NETA CAGI "Netacari, nephew of Cagi"
50	Boleycarrigeen, Kilranelagh, County Wicklow	VOTI "of vote"

CIIC Ref.	Location	Text / Transliteration / Translation
180	Emlagh East, Dingle, County Kerry	BRUSCCOS MAQQI CALIACI "of Bruscus son of Cailech"
193	Maumanorig, County Kerry	ANM COLMAN AILITHIR "[written in] the name of Colmán, the pilgrim"
200	Coolmagort, Dunkerron North, County Kerry	MAQI-TTAL MAQI VORGOS MAQI MUCOI TOICAC "Son of Dal, son of Vergosus (Fergus), son of the tribe of Toica"
300	Old Island, Decies-without-Drum, County Waterford	CUNNETAS MAQI GUC[OI] NETA-SEGAMONAS "Cunnetas, Neta-Segamonas"
317	Aghascrebagh, Upper Strabane, County Tyrone	DOTETTO MAQ[I MAGLANI] "Dotetto, Maglani"

CIIC Ref.	Location	Text / Transliteration / Translation
1082	Ballybroman, County Kerry	GLANNANI MAQI BBRANNAD
1083	Rathkenny, Ardfert, Corkaguiney, County Kerry	COMMAGGAGNI MU[CO]I SAMMNN
—	Ratass Church, Tralee, County Kerry	[A]NM SILLANN MAQ FATTILLOGG

9.3 Wales

Ref.	Location	Text / Transliteration / Translation
423	Castle Villa, Brawdy, Pembrokeshire	Q[--]QA[--]GTE Son of Quegte
426	Bridell, Pembrokeshire	NETTASAGRI MAQI MUCOE BRIACI Nettasagri, Briaci

Ref.	Location	Text / Transliteration / Translation
427	Caldey Island, Penally, Pembrokeshire	MAGL[I]DUBAR [--]QI Magl[ia], Dubr[acunas]
456	Steynton, Pembrokeshire	GENDILI Gendilius

9.4 England

Ref.	Location	Text / Transliteration / Translation
466	Lewannick, Cornwall	IGENAVI MEMOR
467	Lewannick, Cornwall	U[L]CAG[.I] / [.L]CAG[.]I Ulcagni
470	Worthyvale, Slaughterbridge, Minster, Cornwall	LA[TI]NI

Ref.	Location	Text / Transliteration / Translation
484	St. Kew, Cornwall	[I]USTI
489	Fardel Manor, near Ivybridge, Devon	SVAQQUCI MAQI QICI "[The stone] of Safaqqucus, son of Qicus"
488	Roborough Down, Buckland Monachorum, Devon	ENABARR To compare with the name of the horse of Manannan Mac Lir (Enbarr)
496	Silchester, Hampshire	EBICATO[S] [MAQ]I MUCO[I] [

9.5 Isle of Man

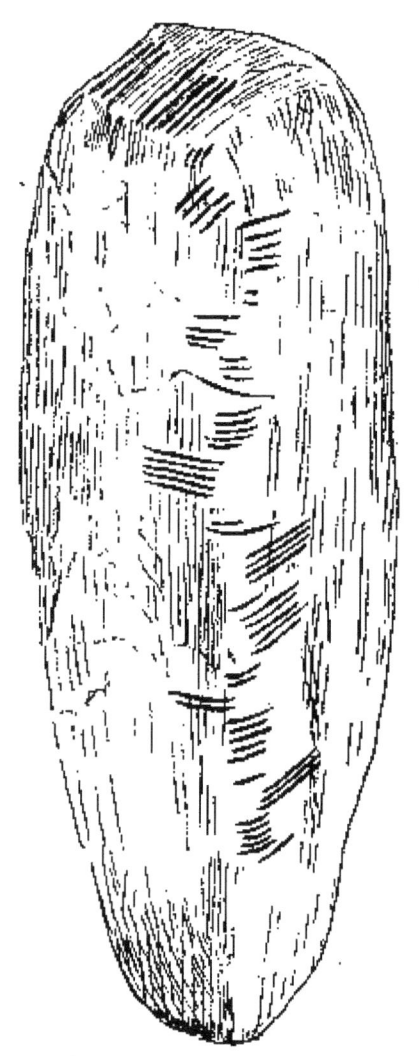

No. 504 Ballaqueeney, Port St Mary, Rushen, Isle of Man
Source: Wikipedia Creative Commons

Ref.	Location	Text / Transliteration / Translation
500	Knoc y Doonee, Kirk Andreas	FILIVS-ROCATI | HIC-IACIT [.]B[I]CATOS-M[A]QI-R[O]C[A]T[O]S "Ammecatus son of Rocatus lies here" "[Am]bicatos son of Rocatos"

Ref.	Location	Text / Transliteration / Translation
501		CUNAMAGLI MAC[
502		MAQ LEOG
503	Ballaqueeney, Port St Mary, Rushen	DOVAIDONA MAQI DROATA "Dovaido son of the Druid".
504	Ballaqueeney, Port St Mary, Rushen	BIVAIDONAS MAQI MUCOI CUNAVA[LI] "Of Bivaidonas, son of the tribe Cunava[li]"

Ogham   *9. Inscriptions*

9.6 Scotland

Newton Stone, Shevock toll-bar, Aberdeenshire
Source: Wikipedia Creative Commons

Ref.	Location	Text / Transliteration / Translation
506	Gigha, Argyll	VICULA MAQ CUGINI Vicula, Cugini
507	Poltaloch, Kilmartin, Argyll	CRON[-][N][
1068	Ballavarkish, Bride	LUGNI

Ref.	Location	Text / Transliteration / Translation
CISP BRATT/1	Brandsbutt, Inverurie, Aberdeenshire	IRATADDOARENS[Addoaren (Saint Ethernan?)
CISP BREAY/1	Bressay, Shetland	CRRO[S]SCC NAHHTVVDDA[DD]S DATTRR [A]NN[--] BEN[I]SES MEQQ DDR[O]ANN[--] Nahhtvdd[add]s, Benises, Dr[o]ann
?	Birsay, Orkney	[B]ENDDACTANIM[L] a blessing on the soul of L.

Ogham   *9. Inscriptions*

Ref.	Location	Text / Transliteration / Translation
?	Auquhollie, near Stonehaven	AVUOANNUNAOUATEDOVENI Avuo Anuano soothsayer of the Doveni
Newton Stone	Shevock toll-bar, Aberdeenshire	AIDDARCUN FEAN FOBRENNI BA(L or K)S IOSSAR

www.ingramcontent.com/pod-product-compliance
Lightning Source LLC
Chambersburg PA
CBHW051422070526
44584CB00023B/3541